# Vividly You(th)

How to Create Your Divine Design

**ANURAG SHARMA**

INDIA • SINGAPORE • MALAYSIA

# Dedication

To the boundless grace of Lord Krishna and the unwavering devotion of Lord Hanuman, whose radiant presence has not only been my guiding light but also the very heartbeat of my existence, illuminating the most profound corners of my soul with their divine love.

And to my beloved parents, my cherished family, and my steadfast friends, whose unwavering love and trust have been the pillars of strength throughout my journey. Your support and belief in me have made this book possible.

# CONTENTS

# FOREWORD

**Forward from Parents**

Dear Readers,

As parents, witnessing the growth and evolution of our children is a journey that fills our hearts with immense joy and pride. Today, we stand here not just as proud parents but as admirers of the extraordinary talent that our son, Anurag, possesses.

The pages you are about to delve into encapsulate the essence of youthful exuberance, dreams, and aspirations. Anurag, with his vivid imagination and unwavering passion, has woven a tapestry of stories that resonate with the essence of youth—its struggles, triumphs, and the vibrant colours that paint this beautiful phase of life.

Anurag's journey as a writer has been one of dedication, perseverance, and unyielding creativity. With each word penned, he has poured his heart and soul into creating a world that reflects the complexities and wonders of being young. His ability to capture the essence of emotions, moments, and the very spirit of youth is nothing short of remarkable.

Through "Vividly Youth," Anurag invites you on a compelling voyage—a journey that will resonate deeply with your own experiences, igniting nostalgia, laughter, and perhaps a few tears along the way. It is a testament to the myriad emotions that define this pivotal stage of life.

We, as his parents, have watched him grow, observed his passion for storytelling blossom, and witnessed his dedication to his craft. We couldn't be prouder to see his dreams come to fruition through these pages. Anurag's commitment to his artistry is evident in every sentence, every chapter, and every character he has brought to life.

As you embark on this literary expedition, we hope you embrace the stories with the same warmth and enthusiasm that Anurag has poured into crafting them. May his words inspire, resonate, and leave an indelible mark on your hearts, just as they have on ours.

Warm regards,

Mr. Ramesh Sharma & Mrs. Madhu Ramesh Sharma

# MY INTENTION TO WRITE THIS BOOK?

The intention behind writing this book is rooted in a profound realization from my own life journey. Through personal experience, I have come to understand the profound significance of key elements in life such as passion, purpose, our actions, and spirituality. Looking back, I often found myself thinking, "I wish I had known these fundamental truths earlier in life." I believe that having this knowledge from the outset could have significantly altered the course of my life, guiding me in a much more purposeful and fulfilling direction.

On the other side of this personal journey, I have evolved into a passionate mentor and coach. My dedication lies in empowering people, especially the dynamic and unique generation known as Gen Z. Through my mentoring interactions, I have intimately witnessed the specific challenges they face and how these challenges can deeply impact their lives and aspirations. It is within these mentoring relationships that a powerful thought was ignited.

With this newfound insight and understanding, I made a conscious and heartfelt intention to offer my support to the new generation. I aim to do so by simplifying and sharing the basic yet profound elements of life. It is my sincere and humble endeavour to provide actionable insights, ones I have gathered through the lessons of my own life, in the hopes of assisting young individuals in their quest to create their own divine design.

In essence, this book is my way of offering guidance and wisdom that I wish I had received when I was at the threshold of my journey. I hope that these insights, shared with love and care, will help the new generation take their first steps towards a life of purpose, fulfilment, and the realization of their divine potential.

# INTRODUCTION

I often find myself overwhelmed with gratitude and a deep sense of fortune for having been born as a part of the remarkable Millennial or Generation Y, a group hailed as the digital natives, spanning from 1982 to 1994. It's a privilege to have witnessed the awe-inspiring evolution of the digital age – from floppy disks to USB drives, and now to the boundless realm of cloud computing. We've moved from the tethered world of wired telephones to the liberating realm of cutting-edge wearables. Our workspaces, once confined to offices, have transcended physical boundaries.

As I reflect on my college days, where I'd tirelessly pour over books to find answers, I'm struck by the present – a time when AI tools like ChatGPT can effortlessly provide instant solutions. This technological revolution, though exhilarating, has also triggered a profound shift in our collective mindset.

Science and engineering are continually moulding our world, paving the way for boundless possibilities. Yet, there are moments when I ponder whether these advances might be driving us apart from society and, more crucially, from ourselves. The mounting distractions are hard to ignore. However, my passion lies in engaging with and nurturing the emerging generation, particularly the brilliant minds of Generation Z. Nonetheless, there's a growing apprehension about certain qualities that seem to be missing in them – patience, perseverance, and a clear sense of purpose. Distractions often sway them, causing them to abandon their goals. It was in response to these concerns that I embarked on a global research journey, and the findings were nothing short of staggering.

- According to Cigna's research, a significant 65% of Gen Z employees have been seriously reevaluating their life priorities in the past two years. Even more astonishing, a whopping 71% of Gen Z individuals find themselves in this contemplative state. Moreover, 34% of Gen Z are anxious about the future, with 24% fearing a scarcity of learning and job opportunities. Despite these concerns, they remain determined, as 48% of Gen Z and Millennials aged 18-35 are planning to embark on new job searches within the next year.

- The data on stress and well-being paints a complex picture. On one hand, the Cigna study shows that 91% of Gen Zs report feeling stressed, with 98% experiencing burnout. Another study by Stress in America finds that 62% of women and 51% of men aged 18-34 are feeling completely overwhelmed by stress. However, there is a glimmer of hope, as a study by Gympass suggests that 59% of Gen Zs have experienced an improvement in their well-being in 2022. Additionally, Gen Zs place a high value on well-being at work, with 78% considering it as important as their salary.

- Engagement appears to be diminishing in an era marked by the rise of remote and hybrid work. Gallup reports that only 32% of people claim to be engaged, with 17% actively disengaged. The Cigna study reveals that Gen Z employees admit to being physically present but not fully engaged for 25% of their work time. Culture is a key factor in the employee experience, with a study by EY finding that 39% of Gen Z workers believe it significantly influences their decision to stay with their current employer. In contrast, the study by Gympass is more optimistic, reporting that 85% of Gen Zs are actively engaged at work.

- Workplace friendships appear to be in crisis, as a study by BetterUp shows that only 31% of people are content with their level of social connection in the workplace. Alarmingly, 22% report having no friends at work. The Cigna study adds to this somber picture, with 48% of Gen Zs feeling that work has become transactional, devoid of opportunities to form bonds with colleagues.

- Financial concerns are also weighing heavily on the minds of Gen Zs. According to the Cigna study, 39% of them attribute significant stress to money worries. Additionally, a study by DailyPay and Harris Poll reveals that 48% believe financial challenges are keeping them in their parents' homes, and 33% fear that inflation will hinder their dreams of homeownership.

All these revelations beg a fundamental question: In a world where everything is at our fingertips, how do we cultivate the resilience needed to conquer challenges? This question impels me to revisit the core values that underpin our progress.

To illuminate the predicament of the next generation, allow me to share a poignant story. In a tranquil village, there resided a farmer who decided to plant two saplings. He showered one with meticulous attention, offering it the finest fertilizer, ample water, and every conceivable comfort. The other sapling received only the essentials, with minimal fuss.

As both plants began to grow, the farmer's daughter watched intently. The first, pampered and nurtured, flourished at an astonishing rate. In contrast, the second, surviving on the bare necessities, made slower progress.

Then, a fierce and unyielding storm swept through the village. After the tempest had passed, the farmer and his daughter hurried to examine the condition of their plants. To the daughter's astonishment, the first plant, the one that had been lavished with care, had not endured the storm. In contrast, the second plant, which had barely received what it needed to survive, had weathered the storm with resilience.

Curiosity piqued, the daughter turned to her father and asked, "Why did the first plant, the one we cared for so lovingly, fail to withstand the storm? And why did the second, which received only the basics, emerge unscathed?"

The farmer's response was profound. He explained that the first plant, accustomed to favourable conditions, had grown complacent. It never needed to develop deep roots or strive to extract what it required from the soil. Consequently, it couldn't withstand the storm's harsh conditions. On the other hand, the second plant, receiving only the essentials, had instinctively recognized the need to grow deeper roots and extract the necessary nutrients for its survival. It had become resilient and robust as a result.

This tale mirrors the situation of today's generation. We are often surrounded by an abundance of resources, conveniences, and digital tools, much like the first plant. This generation has grown up with everything readily available, fostering a sense of entitlement and a penchant for immediate gratification. In such an environment, some individuals may struggle to cultivate the deep roots of patience, perseverance, and a clear sense of purpose.

Conversely, the second plant symbolizes those who have been taught the value of effort and the necessity of extracting what they need from their surroundings.

They've had to adapt, endure challenges, and establish a sturdy foundation. In the face of adversity, they exhibit resilience and resourcefulness, much like the second plant surviving the storm.

The moral of this story is evident: the challenges and hurdles we encounter are not obstacles, but opportunities for growth. Like the second plant, we must cultivate our roots, develop patience, persevere, and nurture a profound sense of purpose. In a world where everything is within reach, it's imperative to remember that genuine strength and resilience emanate from within. The ability to flourish in adversity and attain new heights of accomplishment testifies to the power of perseverance, tenacity, and a clear vision.

The next generation, brimming with brilliance and potential, can draw inspiration from this narrative. It serves as a reminder that the path to success often entails confronting challenges, establishing deep roots, and extracting the vital nutrients of patience and perseverance from life's soil. By doing so, they can develop into individuals of remarkable strength and resilience, capable of enduring any storm that comes their way.

As we traverse the ever-evolving landscape of the digital era, let us not forget the significance of nurturing inner strength, embracing challenges, and instilling in ourselves and the next generation the values of patience, perseverance, and purpose. These qualities, deeply embedded within us, will empower us to flourish in the face of adversity and attain new pinnacles of achievement, much like the second plant that weathered the storm and stood tall.

And so, the book "Vividly You(th): How to Create Your Divine Design" emerges as a guiding beacon for the young individuals navigating the intricate labyrinth of youth. Its purpose is clear: to equip young minds with the fundamentals needed to navigate the complex journey of youth.

This book is organized into distinct sections, each aimed at providing guidance and empowerment to young individuals as they navigate their complex journey. Additionally, it includes a workbook featuring thought-provoking questions for reflection at the end of each key section. The book commences by introducing the concept of the "Labyrinth of Youth."

1. Section One – Clarity of Thoughts: This initial section delves into the significance of clear and focused thinking, offering valuable insights on how to develop and sustain mental clarity amidst the challenges of youth.

2. Section Two – Purity of Heart: In the following section, the book explores the importance of maintaining a pure and open heart. It imparts wisdom on nurturing qualities like empathy, compassion, and emotional well-being during the formative years.

3.  Section Three – Sincerity of Action: The subsequent section emphasizes the value of sincere and purposeful actions. It provides practical guidance on making informed choices, setting goals, and staying committed to one's aspirations.

4.  Section Four – Success Sherpas: Guiding Your Summit with Mentors: This section delves into the topic of mentorship and its significance. It aims to assist young individuals in finding the right mentors to guide them on their journey.

5.  Section Five – Spiritually Conscious: The final section delves into matters of the soul, encouraging spiritual awareness and growth. It guides young individuals in exploring their inner selves and discovering their unique spiritual path.

# THE LABYRINTH OF YOUTH

*"A winding journey where innocence meets experience, and where the footsteps of self-discovery echo in the corridors of time."*

Swami Vivekananda once declared, "I have faith in the young, modern generation. They will navigate life's labyrinth like mighty lions."

In the heart of youth, a labyrinth unfolds – a labyrinth of endless possibilities, challenges, and opportunities. This chapter delves into the ever-changing landscape of youth, exploring the complexities and nuances of this pivotal stage in life. As we begin our journey, we find ourselves at the entrance of a maze, one that often leaves young individuals bewildered, yet brimming with potential.

Youth, that magical and bewildering phase of life, is an ever-changing landscape. It's a stage where one stands on the cusp of adulthood, grappling with the transition from childhood to maturity. This is a period of profound transformation, both physically and emotionally. It's a time when dreams are formed, goals are set, and identities are moulded. It's a time of self-discovery, adventure, and the excitement of the unknown. But it's also a period filled with uncertainty, challenges, and the ever-present question, "Who am I, and where am I going?"

## Defining Youth

Youth is not just a number on the calendar; it's a vibrant state of being a chapter in life defined by a tapestry of shared experiences. While many might place the age range of youth between 15 and 24, the essence of youth transcends mere numbers. It's a realm shaped by culture, geography, the hand you're dealt by circumstance, and the dreams that ignite your soul.

Defining "Youth" is a complex task. For Me It's an energy that courses through your veins, an insatiable hunger for adventure that propels you forward. It's about embracing discipline, becoming a disciple of your own potential, and knowing that you have the power to conquer your inner doubts and fears, rather than letting them conquer you. Youth is a time of unwavering determination, a time when you're poised to take on the world and make your mark.

In the world of young people, there was so much to learn and many tough challenges to face. It was like going on an exciting adventure. Let's explore a few of them.

- **The Digital Age and Its Impact on Youth**

The Digital Age has drastically changed how young people face challenges. They're growing up in a world full of technology, like the internet, smartphones, and social media. This technology has altered the way they interact with others, learn, and see themselves and the world. While the digital world offers lots of opportunities, it also brings its own problems, like always comparing themselves to others online and feeling pressured to fit in.

Let's take a look at Surabhi, an 18-year-old high school student. She spends most of her day online, using social media and her smartphone to stay in touch with friends, family, and schoolmates. It's like a portal to a world of information and fun.

But under the surface, Surabhi faces some unique challenges. In the Digital Age, there's a flood of content online, and much of it is carefully chosen to show a perfect life. This can make Sarah feel like her life isn't good enough. She also feels like she has to be online all the time, responding to messages and notifications right away.

Studies show that Surabhi 's experiences are not unusual. For instance, a study by the Pew Research Center found that 81% of teenagers use social media, where people often post carefully selected pictures and updates. This can create unrealistic standards and make young people doubt themselves, just like Surabhi.

Another study by Common Sense Media revealed that 72% of teenagers feel the need to reply to messages and notifications instantly. Surabhi is not alone in this; many young people struggle to find a balance between their online and offline lives because they are always connected.

In short, the Digital Age has introduced new challenges for young people, like constantly comparing themselves to others online and feeling the pressure to fit in. These challenges affect many young individuals, shaping the way they see the world.

- **Identity Formation in Youth**

The years of youth are a critical period for identity development. It's the time when individuals confront questions about their own identity and aspirations for the future. This phase involves self-discovery, as young people explore their interests, values, and beliefs. The quest for one's identity can be empowering, yet it often brings about uncertainty as young individuals experiment with various aspects of themselves.

To illustrate this process, let's dive into a story that exemplifies the challenges and complexities of identity formation in youth.

Meet Alex, a 17-year-old high school student. Alex has always been a star athlete, excelling in various sports, and that's how everyone knows them. However, deep down, Alex has been nurturing a passion for music. They've been quietly learning to play the guitar and writing songs in their spare time. This hidden talent feels like a secret part of their identity that he haven't yet shared with friends or family.

As Alex grapples with their burgeoning interest in music, they face an internal conflict. He feel tied to their athletic image and fear that embracing their musical side might lead to judgment or disappointment from others. This internal struggle is a common aspect of identity formation, where young people must balance societal expectations with their genuine passions and interests.

Research supports Alex's journey. According to a study by the National Institute of Child Health and Human Development, identity formation in adolescence is a critical process, often marked by experimentation and self-discovery. It's during this time that young individuals explore various aspects of themselves, attempting to find congruence between their inner desires and societal roles.

Furthermore, a survey by the American Psychological Association highlights that adolescents often experience a sense of identity crisis, grappling with questions like "Who am I?" and "What do I want to be?" This period of exploration can be both exciting and perplexing as young people strive to create a cohesive self-concept.

In essence, youth is a pivotal phase where identity takes shape. It's a time of self-discovery and experimentation, often characterized by internal conflicts as young individuals endeavour to balance societal expectations with their authentic passions and interests. This journey, like Alex's, is a common experience for many as they navigate the complex terrain of identity formation.

- **Navigating Societal Expectations in Youth: A Tale from India**

In the context of India's society, there is a well-defined set of expectations for young people. These expectations often revolve around academic excellence, the pursuit of a stable and prestigious career, and the formation of traditional relationships. The weight of conformity to these societal norms can be overwhelming, making it difficult for young individuals to carve out their own distinctive paths and follow their true desires.

Let's delve into the story of Raj, a 20-year-old student in India, to better illustrate the challenges associated with societal expectations.

Raj, like many Indian youth, has grown up with the notion that academic success is the key to a prosperous future. His parents, like those of many of his friends, have invested significant time and resources in his education, with high hopes for him to become a successful engineer or doctor. Raj is a diligent student, scoring well in his science courses, but he secretly harbours a passion for art. He's a talented painter and often finds solace in expressing himself through his artwork.

Raj's story highlights the dilemma faced by numerous young Indians. The pressure to excel academically and pursue a career in science or medicine is immense, and Raj feels it keenly. His parents, while well-intentioned, unknowingly add to his burden by emphasizing the importance of a stable, well-paying job. This societal expectation leaves Raj with a difficult choice – to follow his passion for art or to conform to the expectations of a more conventional career path.

Research into the challenges of societal expectations on Indian youth underscores Raj's predicament. According to a survey conducted by the National Youth Policy, many young people in India struggle with balancing their own aspirations with those of their families and communities. The pressure to meet traditional standards can result in internal conflict, and the fear of disappointing loved ones is a significant emotional burden.

Furthermore, data from the Youth in India: Situation and Needs study by the United Nations Population Fund (UNFPA) reveals that the pressure to marry at a certain age and adhere to traditional gender roles is another facet of societal expectations faced by Indian youth. These expectations can limit the freedom of young people to make choices that align with their personal values and desires.

The story of Raj represents the challenges many young Indians face when trying to reconcile their personal aspirations with societal norms. Research findings show that these pressures can result in internal conflict and hinder the ability of young people to make choices that resonate with their individual values and dreams.

- **Navigating Life's Crossroads: A Global and Indian Perspective on Youth Challenges**

Youth is a pivotal phase marked by an abundance of choices, and the burden to make the "right" decisions can weigh heavily on young shoulders. The fear of making errors or letting others down can loom over the decision-making process, and the ambiguity of what lies ahead can be paralyzing. It is crucial for young individuals to recognize that making mistakes is a natural part of life, and that life itself is a continual learning journey.

To better understand the challenges of making choices, let's explore two stories—one from a global perspective and another from India.

**The Global Story: Maria's Dilemma**

Meet Maria, a 22-year-old from Brazil. She has just graduated from university and is standing at a crossroads. The pressure to find a prestigious job, earn a good income, and meet societal expectations is immense. Maria's parents, like many others, have invested in her education with high hopes for her future success. However, Maria yearns to travel the world and explore different cultures before settling into a traditional career.

The global landscape reflects Maria's dilemma. According to a report by the International Labour Organization (ILO), global youth unemployment rates remain high, and young people often feel compelled to secure stable employment swiftly. The pressure to meet societal expectations can be a significant challenge, making it tough for young individuals like Maria to follow their passions and unconventional dreams.

## The Indian Story: Arjun's Struggle

Now, let's turn our attention to Arjun, a 19-year-old student from India. In India, academic success is deeply ingrained in societal expectations, and Arjun's parents have high hopes for him to become an engineer. However, Arjun's true passion lies in literature. He dreams of becoming a writer and nurturing his love for storytelling.

The challenge Arjun faces is all too familiar in the Indian context. According to a survey by the National Youth Policy, many Indian youth encounter difficulties in pursuing their own aspirations when these aspirations diverge from traditional career paths. The fear of disappointing family and society often takes precedence over personal dreams, making it challenging for young people like Arjun to make choices that genuinely resonate with their hearts.

In essence, the phase of youth is laden with choices, and the pressure to make the "right" decisions is a universal experience. Both globally and in India, the fear of making mistakes and the weight of societal expectations can be daunting. It is vital for young individuals to understand that making mistakes is part of life's learning process, and that their personal journeys may not always align with the expectations of others.

- **Navigating Life's Maze**

Imagine being at the entrance of a maze, a place full of twists, turns, and choices. Youth often feels like exploring this complex puzzle, with lots of unexpected challenges. It's a time when you have to make important decisions that will affect your future, like choosing a career, deciding on education, and building personal relationships.

To understand these challenges better, let's Meet Rahul, an 18-year-old from New Delhi, India. He's just finished high school and faces some big decisions. One of the most crucial is picking a college major. In India, this choice carries a lot of weight because it not only determines what you study but also plays a big role in your future career.

Rahul's story is a common one in India. Young people often feel the pressure to make the "right" career choice, influenced by what society and their families expect. According to data from the National Sample Survey Office in India, more young people are going to college, which is great, but it also means more competition for the best courses and careers.

In India, relationships can also be a tricky part of the maze. With a strong tradition of arranged marriages, young people like Rahul might struggle to balance tradition with their personal choices when it comes to love and relationships.

In short, navigating through youth is like finding your way through a maze with lots of paths and choices. Young people, especially in India, face significant decisions that can shape their lives, like what to study and what career to pursue. Rahul's story is a reflection of the challenges many young Indians face as they make their way through this complex maze of life's complexities.

The labyrinth of youth is a multifaceted terrain, where each individual's path is unique. It's a phase filled with promise, discovery, and growth, but it's also riddled with challenges, ambiguity, and external pressures. As we embark on our journey through this labyrinth, it's essential to acknowledge its complexities and embrace the uncertainty that comes with it.

# CLARITY OF THOUGHTS

*"Clarity of thought illuminates the path to purpose
and fuels the fire of achievement."*

WHEN YOU'RE YOUNG, life can feel like a big, messy wave crashing around you. You're full of strong feelings and don't always know where you're going. Let me tell you a story about a young person named Lily. She lived near the ocean, and her life was a lot like the sea. It could be calm and beautiful one moment, and then wild and scary the next.

Lily had big dreams. She wanted to study the amazing creatures in the ocean and become a marine biologist. But there were many things making her feel unsure and lost. She had to deal with school pressure and what others expected of her.

One sunny day, as Lily sat by the ocean, she saw how the waves represented her own messy thoughts and feelings. Just like the sea changed from calm to stormy, her life had its ups and downs. She realized that to reach her dreams, she needed to clear her mind and find a way through the confusion.

Lily's journey to clarity was a lot like finding a lighthouse to guide her through the stormy sea of youth. This section is about journey of millions youth like lily and how they can find clarity, too.

## Inner game equation: Zeal, Intent, Realism

Every single day, as we wake up and reach for our devices, we are bombarded with motivational messages on social media platforms like Instagram, YouTube, and LinkedIn. They all seem to echo the same sentiment: Follow Your Passion, disappear for six months to follow your dream, do what makes you happy, and ask the burning question, "What are you waiting for? Go get your dream." These messages often come in the form of posts, videos, and reels, designed to trigger that rush of dopamine we all love. While these messages are inspiring, they tend to oversimplify the path to success.

In reality, achieving our dreams is a multifaceted journey that requires more than just unbridled enthusiasm. It demands vision, preparation, strategy, and the presence of a support system. Blindly pursuing your dreams without a clear plan can lead to a mess of confusion and frustration. The process is not as simple as it may seem on the surface.

In the quest for success, we must remember that every step counts. It's not just about pursuing our passion; it's about doing so with purpose. We need a holistic approach, an equation that encapsulates the essence of achieving our dreams:

**Your Reality + Your Purpose * Your Intent + Your Zeal = A Step Towards Your Dream**

To break it down further, let's explore each component of this equation in more depth.

**Your Reality**

Reality is the ground on which your dreams must be built. It's the practical aspects of life that cannot be ignored. This includes your current circumstances, responsibilities, and limitations. While it's important to dream big, it's equally crucial to face your reality. Understanding your reality helps you make informed decisions and adapt your plan to fit your life. Ignoring reality can lead to disappointment and setbacks.

**Your Purpose * Your Intent**

While zeal is a critical component of achieving our dreams, it is not enough on its own. To effectively harness the power of zeal, we must pair it with intent and purpose. Intent is the clarity of our goals and the determination to achieve them, while purpose is the underlying reason that drives us forward.

Intent involves setting clear, well-defined objectives and making a conscious decision to work towards them. It is the deliberate action of mapping out our goals and creating a plan to achieve them. Intent provides the direction and focus needed to channel our zeal effectively. Without intent, zeal can become scattered, leading to unproductive efforts.

Purpose, on the other hand, is the "why" behind our dreams. It is the deeply rooted reason that fuels our passion and commitment. Purpose provides meaning to our goals and gives them a sense of significance. When we have a strong sense of purpose, our zeal becomes a force to be reckoned with, as it is driven by a profound connection to our dreams and a desire to make a positive impact on the world.

**Your Zeal**

Zeal is the driving force that propels us toward our dreams and goals. It is the unshakeable enthusiasm that keeps us moving forward, even when faced with challenges. Zeal is the inner fire that burns brightly, providing us with the energy and determination required to persevere in the pursuit of our dreams. It is the voice of our higher self, constantly reminding us of our potential and urging us to push beyond our limits.

When we possess zeal, our hearts are filled with a sense of purpose and excitement. We wake up each day with a fervent desire to make our dreams a reality. This unwavering enthusiasm gives us the strength to weather the storms of life and keep pushing forward, regardless of the obstacles that may come our way. Zeal is the raw material for our dreams, the powerful force that fuels our ambition and sets us on a path to success. While zeal is a critical component of achieving our dreams, it is not enough on its own. To effectively harness the power of zeal, we must pair it with intent and purpose.

## The Synergy of Zeal, Intent, and Purpose

The synergy of zeal, intent, and purpose is the key to achieving our dreams. Zeal provides the initial burst of energy and enthusiasm, driving us to take action. Intent offers the structure and strategy to move us in the right direction, ensuring that our efforts are focused and effective. Purpose infuses our journey with meaning and determination, keeping us committed to our goals even when challenges arise.

When we combine zeal, intent, and purpose, we create a powerful formula for success. Zeal provides the passion and excitement that fuels our journey, intent offers the roadmap to guide us, and purpose gives us the unwavering determination to press on. With this combination, we are equipped to overcome obstacles, adapt to changing circumstances, and stay true to our dreams.

## How to put this equation into action

At the start, grasping your true passions and purpose can be challenging. To kickstart this journey, it's beneficial to begin with the concept of "Reality." This step is crucial in navigating life's path, helping you make sense of your current circumstances.

## Your Reality

Reality serves as your anchor, grounding you in the unadorned truth of the world. It's a clear view of things as they are, free from the influence of imagination, wishful thinking, or distortion. It involves recognizing the present moment, objectively assessing your situation, and accepting that life often unfolds beyond our complete control.

Understanding reality means aligning with the actual facts and limitations of your surroundings and your life. It's about embracing "what is" instead of fixating on "what if."

### Why is Reality Important?

The importance of embracing reality is multifold:

### 1. Effective Decision-Making

In the intricate web of life, decision-making is the thread that weaves our past, present, and future together. When we perceive reality accurately, we gain the insights needed to make choices that harmonize with our goals and values. Consider this: Imagine you're at a crossroads, unsure whether to pursue a new career opportunity. Embracing reality allows you to assess the situation objectively. You weigh the pros and cons, considering your skills, interests, and personal values. With this clear understanding, you make an informed decision that resonates with your authentic self.

In contrast, misguided choices often arise from false assumptions or an unwillingness to confront the truth. These choices lead us down paths that deviate from our aspirations. By embracing reality, we navigate our life journey with a compass that always points us in the right direction.

## 2. Resilience

Resilience is the steel within us that flexes and bends but never breaks. It's our ability to withstand the storms of life and emerge stronger. Embracing reality is the cornerstone of resilience. When we confront adversity with a clear understanding of the challenges, we empower ourselves to adapt and overcome. Picture a resilient oak tree in a fierce storm. Its deep roots anchor it firmly, while its branches sway with the wind. The tree doesn't resist the storm; it endures and adapts. Similarly, when we acknowledge the reality of a situation, we can adapt our strategies and persevere. This is the essence of resilience.

## 3. Contentment

In our fast-paced world, contentment often eludes us as we chase dreams and aspirations. However, contentment is not the absence of ambition; it is the acceptance of the present moment. Embracing reality grounds, us in the here and now, nurturing contentment.

Think of a serene pond reflecting the surrounding trees. The pond doesn't yearn to become a river or a lake; it is content being a pond. When we appreciate what is, rather than yearning for what isn't, we find peace in the current moment. Embracing reality brings a profound sense of contentment, making each day a gift rather than a stepping stone to an elusive future.

## 4. Honest Relationships

Our lives are interwoven with relationships, both personal and professional. Authenticity is the bedrock of these connections, and authenticity is based on an understanding of reality. When we are genuine and transparent about who we are and what we believe, trust blossoms, and open communication flourishes.

Imagine two friends who are unafraid to share their thoughts and feelings. Their relationship is built on trust, with each person embracing the other's reality. They accept each other's flaws and appreciate their strengths. This honesty deepens their bond, making their friendship resilient and fulfilling.

Conversely, when we hide our true selves or avoid confronting uncomfortable truths, our relationships become fragile and strained. Embracing reality in relationships, including acknowledging differences and addressing conflicts, fosters trust, understanding, and a sense of connection that is both authentic and enduring.

## 5. Resource Optimization

Life is a canvas, and our resources are the colours with which we paint our masterpiece. Resource optimization is about making the most of what we have. Recognizing your available resources, such as time, energy, and skills, allows you to allocate them effectively, optimizing your life and pursuits.

Consider your time as a precious resource. Embracing reality means acknowledging the reality of your 24-hour day. By recognizing the constraints of time, you can make choices that prioritize what truly matters. This results in greater productivity, a sense of accomplishment, and a life well-lived.

Similarly, by understanding your skills and energy levels, you can allocate them where they will have the most significant impact. Embracing reality helps you paint your life's canvas with precision and artistry, creating a picture that is both vibrant and harmonious.

## How to Create Your Reality

To grasp a simple principle, consider the essence of energy in the words we speak, the thoughts we harbour, the beliefs we embrace, and everything we undertake. Each of these components carries an energy, akin to a vibe. This energy serves as a message dispatched into the universe, summoning circumstances that resonate with our energetic signals. Our inner world inevitably manifests in the external reality, molding our life experiences.

Empowering change within our reality lies within our control, given our capacity to alter our energy. To shape your reality, focus on these five fundamental aspects:

a. **Language:** Be mindful of the words you use. Are they positive or negative? Employ positive words to invite favourable outcomes.

b. **Thoughts:** Stay conscious of your thoughts. Are you fixating on your desires or dwelling on what you wish to avoid? Channel your thoughts toward your aspirations.

c. **Beliefs:** Your beliefs dictate your perceived reality. Foster beliefs that affirm the arrival of positive circumstances.

d. **Emotions:** Your emotions hold considerable influence. Cultivate feelings of happiness, excitement, and confidence, as these emotions attract positive outcomes.

e. **Actions:** Your actions play a pivotal role. Align your actions with the reality you wish to create.

In order to focus on these five fundamental aspects, one must Start with Satisfaction: The first step to changing your energy is to be happy and satisfied with what you have. When you're content, you start attracting good things.

It's important to be mindful of the influences you permit in your life. This includes the people you spend time with, the content you consume, the thoughts you entertain, and the beliefs and emotions you hold. These factors all contribute to the reality you shape.

**Workbook Reflection Time – Life is all about powerful questioning.**

1.  List five things you're grateful for today.

2.  Record the words and phrases you use most often in your daily life.

3.  Visualize yourself on the big screen of life. Consider your beliefs about relationships and finances.

4.  Write down the names of five people who are most precious to you.

5.  Identify three areas where you invest the most time and note what brings you joy and sadness in those areas.

6.  Define your strengths, fears, and areas for improvement.

7.  Reflect on the information you've gathered and identify five areas of life that matter most to you, such as Health, Relationships, Career, Finance, etc. Rate your current and desired situations in each area and set short-term goals to bridge the gap.

In summary, embracing reality is not a passive acceptance of life's circumstances; it is an active engagement with the world as it is. By embracing reality, you empower yourself to make effective decisions, cultivate resilience, find contentment, nurture honest relationships, and optimize your resources. This practice, when combined with Purpose and intent, enables you to shape a life that is authentic, purposeful, and fulfilling.

## Your Purpose and Intent

Purpose and intent serve as the guiding stars that steer the course of your life's journey. Purpose represents the overarching "why" behind your existence, while intent comprises the focused and deliberate actions you take to progress toward your purpose. Together, they offer a roadmap for your actions, light the way through life's complexities, and supply the impetus to persevere.

Purpose is the grand, It encapsulates your deepest values, desires, and long-term objectives. Your purpose is the foundation upon which you build your life, setting the stage for your actions and choices. It's the profound answer to the question, "What am I here to achieve?" Purpose gives life meaning and significance, infusing your daily endeavors with a sense of direction.

Intent, on the other hand, zooms in on the micro-level. It embodies the specific, deliberate actions you take to advance your purpose. Intent is the force that propels you forward, one step at a time, on your journey towards fulfilling your purpose. It serves as a powerful motivator, ensuring that your daily decisions and activities are aligned with your greater mission.

When both purpose and intent are firmly grounded in reality, they become even more influential. It's in the tangible world that your dreams take shape, and it's through real actions that you make progress. Purpose and intent, when tethered to the realities of your circumstances, become potent forces for transformation. Your purpose remains rooted in what's achievable, while your intent breaks down the grand vision into manageable steps.

**Why are Purpose and Intent Important?**

**1. Clarity in Chaos**

Life is a complex and often chaotic journey. It throws unexpected challenges and uncertainties our way. In this whirlwind, purpose and intent serve as our guiding lights, like a compass in the storm. They offer clarity, a sense of direction, and meaning in the midst of chaos.

Imagine sailing through a turbulent sea without any navigational aids. You'd be lost, tossed about by the waves, and unsure of your destination. Similarly, in life, without a clear purpose and intent, you may find yourself adrift, uncertain of where you're heading. However, when you have a defined purpose and intent, they act as a compass, providing a sense of direction and helping you navigate through life's turbulence.

Having a purpose and intent doesn't eliminate the chaos or challenges; it provides a framework for dealing with them. It's like knowing that your ultimate goal is to reach a certain island on your voyage. Even if you encounter storms, you'll adjust your course, persevere through difficulties, and stay focused on reaching your destination.

## 2. Motivation and Resilience

A clear purpose and intent are not only about knowing where you're going but also about the motivation to get there. They serve as powerful motivators, fueling your determination and resilience.

Think of motivation as the wind in your sails. With a strong wind, you'll move swiftly towards your destination. In life, your purpose and intent are that wind. They provide the energy and enthusiasm to keep going, even when faced with challenges. When your purpose is deeply meaningful to you, and your intent is crystal clear, you'll find an inner drive that keeps you going, regardless of the obstacles in your path.

Resilience, too, is closely tied to purpose and intent. When you know why you're on your journey and what you intend to achieve, setbacks and obstacles become stepping stones rather than roadblocks. You bounce back from failures because your purpose gives you a reason to persist. The clearer your intent, the more resilient you become.

## 3. Alignment with Reality

Crafting your purpose and intent based on the reality you've embraced ensures that your goals are attainable and in harmony with your capabilities. This alignment with reality is crucial for long-term success and fulfilment.

Imagine setting sail for an island that's beyond the reach of your ship. No matter how strong your purpose or how clear your intent, you won't reach your destination. In life, aligning your purpose and intent with your capabilities is like choosing a destination that's within your reach.

Sometimes, our aspirations can be unrealistic, leading to disappointment and frustration. However, when we ground our purpose and intent in reality, we set ourselves up for success. It's about recognizing your strengths and limitations and shaping your goals accordingly. This doesn't mean you should set small or easily achievable goals. It means you should aim high while staying rooted in what's possible for you.

Alignment with reality also involves being aware of the external factors that may influence your journey. These can include economic conditions, social dynamics, and personal circumstances. By understanding these factors and adapting your purpose and intent to the ever-changing landscape, you increase your chances of success.

## 4. Fulfilment

Purpose and intent are not just practical tools for navigating life; they also infuse your journey with meaning and fulfilment. They provide a reason to get out of bed in the morning and drive your actions with purpose.

Imagine waking up every day without a sense of purpose or direction. You might find it difficult to muster the enthusiasm to face the day's challenges. But when you have a clear purpose and intent, you wake up with a sense of purpose. You know why you're doing what you're doing, and that knowledge energizes you.

Fulfilment in life often comes from knowing that your actions have meaning and contribute to a larger purpose. It's the satisfaction that comes from working toward your goals and achieving them. Purpose and intent are the driving forces behind this sense of fulfilment. They turn daily tasks into meaningful steps on your journey, making every moment valuable.

## 5. Effective Decision-Making

Purpose and intent guide your decision-making process. When you know your overarching goals, it becomes easier to choose actions that lead you in the right direction. In essence, your purpose and intent act as a filter for your decisions, helping you prioritize what matters most.

Consider decision-making as a series of forks in the road during your journey. Each choice you make takes you down a different path. Without purpose and intent, these choices may seem arbitrary or based on short-term desires. However, when you have a clear purpose and intent, your decisions become intentional and goal-oriented.

Your purpose helps you determine which path aligns with your ultimate destination. It's like having a map that shows you the route to your goal. Your intent ensures that your choices are consistent with your objectives. It's like a signpost that keeps you on the right track.

Moreover, purpose and intent provide a framework for evaluating the consequences of your decisions. They help you consider the long-term effects of your choices and make decisions that are in line with your values and aspirations. This results in a more coherent and purpose-driven life.

Purpose and intent are not mere abstract concepts but practical tools for leading a meaningful and purpose-driven life.

## How to discover your own purpose and intent

Discovering your own purpose and intent is like finding the guiding star of your life. It's a process of digging deep within yourself, exploring various avenues, and staying open to change. Here's a detailed guide on how to embark on this journey:

**1. Self-Reflection** – The Mirror of Your Soul: Begin by taking some quiet moments to look inwards. Think about what really matters to you. Consider your values, the things that ignite your passion, and activities that bring you joy and fulfilment. Ask yourself, "What issues in the world resonate with me?" A helpful tool to uncover your strengths is the Johari Window, which divides your self-awareness into four quadrants:

- **Open Self:** What you and others know about you.

- **Blind Self:** What others know about you, but you're unaware of.

- **Hidden Self:** What you know about yourself, but others don't.

- **Unknown Self:** What neither you nor others know.

**2. Set Clear Goals** – The Blueprint of Your Purpose: Your purpose often emerges from the goals you set. Make sure your goals align with your values and give you a sense of direction. To clarify your intent, consider using frameworks like OKR (Objectives and Key Results) and 5Rs (Result, Responsibility, Resources, Rewards, and Risk).

**3. Explore and Experiment** – The Adventure of Discovery: Don't fear the unknown. Trying new things and venturing down different paths can help you uncover your true passions. It's perfectly fine to change course as you learn more about yourself and your interests.

**4. Seek Inspiration** – Learning from the Wise: Read inspiring books, listen to motivating talks, and connect with people who have already found their purpose. Learning from others' experiences can offer valuable insights and ignite your own motivation.

**5. Mindfulness and Meditation** – A Journey Within: These practices can help you connect with your inner self. They reduce distractions and provide clarity about your desires and aspirations. Think of them as your compass to navigate the sea of your thoughts.

**6. Talk to a Coach or Mentor** – Guiding Lights: If you're struggling to discover your purpose, consider seeking help from a professional coach or Mentor. They possess the knowledge and techniques to support you on your journey.

**7. Keep Learning** – The Path to Self-Discovery: Lifelong learning and personal growth are crucial. The more you learn and grow, the better you'll understand your interests and passions. It's like adding pieces to the puzzle of your life.

**8. Stay Open-Minded** – Embrace Change: Be open to the idea that your purpose and intent may evolve over time. Just as life changes, so can your guiding star. Stay flexible and adaptable as you move forward.

Remember, discovering your purpose and intent is a personal voyage, and there's no fixed timeline. Be patient with yourself and enjoy the process of self-discovery. Your purpose is like a hidden treasure waiting to be unearthed, and every step you take brings you closer to uncovering it.

**Workbook Reflection Time – Life is all about powerful questioning.**

**1. What Ignites Your Passion?**

- What activities or topics make you feel most alive and enthusiastic?

- When was the last time you felt truly passionate about something, and what were you doing at that moment?

- Reflect on the times in your life when you've felt a deep sense of purpose. What were the common elements in those experiences?

**2. What Are Your Core Values?**

- What values are most important to you in life? (e.g., honesty, family, creativity, freedom)

- Can you recall a time when you compromised on your values? How did it make you feel, and what did you learn from that experience?

- How might your values guide you in making important life decisions?

**3. What Impact Do You Want to Make?**

- Imagine your ideal future. What kind of impact or legacy do you want to leave on the world?

- Who are the people or communities you want to positively affect, and how do you envision doing that?

- Consider your strengths and talents. How can you leverage them to create a lasting impact?

## 4. What Are Your Strengths and Weaknesses?

- What are your unique strengths, talents, and skills that set you apart?

- What are some areas where you feel less confident or competent? How might you work on improving these weaknesses or leveraging them differently?

- How can you use your strengths to align with your purpose and overcome any obstacles that stand in your way?

## 5. What Brings You Joy and Fulfilment?

- Think about the moments in your life when you felt the happiest and most fulfilled. What were you doing, and who were you with?

- Are there recurring themes or activities that consistently bring you joy? How can you incorporate more of them into your daily life?

- What small steps can you take to infuse more joy and fulfilment into your daily routines and long-term goals?

## Your Zeal

Once you have a clear understanding of your reality (what's going on around you), your purpose (what you want to achieve), and your intent (your plan to achieve it), it's time to bring in the powerful force of zeal. Zeal is like the fire that starts your journey, gives you the energy to take action, and pushes you forward with a lot of excitement.

Zeal is like the energy that makes your purpose and plan work. It makes your actions full of passion and a strong commitment.

## Reasons Why Zeal Matters in Your Journey

Here are three important reasons why zeal is a crucial element in your journey:

### 1. Sustained Motivation

Imagine setting out on a challenging journey, full of obstacles and uncertainties. At the outset, your excitement and determination are high. However, as you progress, you encounter roadblocks and difficulties that can easily demotivate you. This is where zeal comes into play.

Zeal is the unwavering enthusiasm that keeps you motivated even when faced with obstacles. It serves as a wellspring of energy, ensuring you stay focused on your goals. When the initial enthusiasm wanes, zeal acts as a reserve of passion, reminding you why you started the journey in the first place.

Think of it as a reserve of inner strength. It's what prevents you from giving up when the going gets tough. With zeal, you can tap into a deep well of motivation, enabling you to persevere even in the face of adversity.

## 2. Creative Innovation

Another vital aspect of zeal is its role in fostering creativity and innovation. When you're zealous about your journey, you're more likely to think outside the box, explore new possibilities, and find creative solutions to challenges.

Zeal encourages you to take risks and experiment with different approaches. It empowers you to break free from conventional thinking and seek innovative ways to overcome obstacles. This willingness to explore uncharted territory can lead to groundbreaking ideas and fresh perspectives.

Consider zeal as the catalyst for creative thinking. It fuels your imagination, enabling you to see opportunities where others might only see problems. With a zealous mindset, you become a problem solver, unafraid to confront difficulties and turn them into opportunities for growth.

## 3. Resilience

Life is full of ups and downs, and your journey is no exception. Setbacks and adversities are inevitable, but it's how you respond to them that matters. Zeal provides the resilience needed to weather these storms.

Zeal fuels your determination to persevere through difficult times. When faced with a setback, it doesn't let you give up; instead, it stirs a burning desire to overcome challenges. This resilience is a valuable asset, as it helps you bounce back stronger than before.

Think of zeal as your shield against discouragement. It reminds you of your unwavering commitment to your journey and your purpose. With zeal, you develop the mental toughness needed to withstand adversity and emerge on the other side with newfound strength and wisdom.

## How to cultivate and harness Zeal

Zeal, that powerful force of unwavering enthusiasm, is a key ingredient in your journey towards success. To cultivate and harness this vital energy, follow these actionable steps:

### 1. Embrace Your Purpose:

Zeal is intimately connected to your sense of purpose. The stronger your connection to your goals and the reasons driving your journey, the easier it is to kindle your zeal. Take time for introspection and consider the following framework:

- **Reflect:** Spend time contemplating your purpose and the "why" behind your journey. Ask yourself what truly matters to you.

- **Define Your Goals:** Clearly articulate your objectives. What are you striving to achieve, and why is it important to you?

- **Create a Vision Statement:** Craft a concise statement that embodies your purpose and goals. This statement will serve as a constant reminder of your mission.

## 2. Envision Success:

Visualization can be a potent tool for rekindling your zeal. When you can vividly see the positive outcomes waiting at the end of your path, your enthusiasm is reignited. Here's a framework to help you harness this power:

- **Create a Mental Image:** Close your eyes and vividly picture your journey's success. What does it look, feel, and sound like?

- **Practice Regularly:** Set aside time each day for visualization. The more you practice, the more real and compelling your vision becomes.

- **Positive Affirmations:** Accompany your visualization with positive affirmations that reinforce your belief in achieving success.

## 3. Seek Inspiration:

To maintain your zeal, seek inspiration from diverse sources. Whether it's books, mentors, or like-minded individuals, these sources can fuel your passion. Use this framework to gather inspiration effectively:

- **Diversify Your Sources:** Explore a variety of mediums, from books and articles to podcasts and documentaries. Seek out content that resonates with your journey.

- **Identify Role Models:** Identify individuals who have achieved what you aspire to accomplish. Study their stories and learn from their experiences.

- **Build a Support Network:** Surround yourself with people who share your passion and enthusiasm. Engage in meaningful conversations and exchange ideas.

## 4. Celebrate Small Victories:

Acknowledging and celebrating your small wins along the way is a powerful motivator that sustains your zeal. Follow this framework to effectively celebrate your achievements:

- **Set Milestones:** Divide your journey into smaller, achievable milestones. Each milestone becomes an opportunity for celebration.

- **Reward Yourself:** Establish a system of rewards for reaching these milestones. This can be as simple as treating yourself to something you enjoy.

- **Reflect and Reinforce:** After celebrating, take a moment to reflect on the progress made and remind yourself of the bigger picture.

## 5. Embrace a Growth Mindset:

In the face of challenges and setbacks, adopting a growth mindset can help maintain your enthusiasm. Use this framework to develop a mindset focused on continuous improvement:

- **Welcome Challenges:** Embrace obstacles as opportunities for growth. Rather than viewing them as roadblocks, see them as stepping stones to success.

- **Learn and Adapt:** After facing a setback, analyze what went wrong and what you've learned from the experience. Use this knowledge to adjust your approach.

- **Stay Resilient:** Remind yourself that setbacks are temporary and can lead to personal and professional development. Your resilience in the face of adversity will fuel your zeal.

**Workbook Reflection Time – Life is all about powerful questioning**

**1. What Makes You Feel Super Excited?**

- List activities or things that make you really, really happy.

- When you do them, you can't stop smiling.

**2. When Do You Forget About Time?**

- Think about moments when you were so busy having fun that you didn't even notice the hours passing.

- What were you doing during those times?

**3. What Problems Do You Want to Solve?**

- What issues or challenges are important to you?

- List the things you'd love to make better in the world.

# PURITY OF HEART

*"Emotions are the vibrant colours of our inner world, and a pure heart is the canvas on which they paint the masterpiece of our existence".*

In the relentless struggle that life often presents, it is easy to get entangled in the web of our own ambitions, fears, and desires. The constant fight with the world can consume us, making us forget about the emotions of both others and ourselves. In this chapter, we delve into the profound significance of a pure and open heart, shedding light on how emotions and purity of heart are integral to achieving genuine success and creating lasting happiness.

## Mirage of Absolute Clarity

Imagine absolute clarity as a crystal-clear goal in life, something many people want to achieve. It's like a beautiful vision of a world where everything makes perfect sense, where logic and reason rule. But here's the catch: as we chase this perfect clarity, we often discover it's like a mirage in the desert, always just out of reach. The more we try to grasp it, the more it fades away.

While having a clear purpose and direction is important, going too far in pursuit of absolute clarity can cause us to lose touch with our feelings and emotions. It's like getting so focused on the destination that we forget to enjoy the journey, to experience all the different emotions and connections that make life rich and meaningful. In simpler terms, it's a reminder that emotions and human values are important and shouldn't be neglected in the quest for perfect clarity.

## Emotions: The Colours of Life

Imagine life as a beautiful canvas waiting to be painted, and emotions are the colors an artist uses to make it vibrant and rich. Just like how an artist creates a masterpiece with a palette full of colors, our emotions add depth and variety to our journey through life. These emotions are like the raw materials that shape our experiences and how we connect with the world.

You might have experienced different emotions, like happiness, sadness, anger, and love. They're like the reds, blues, and yellows on an artist's palette. Emotions can be powerful and intense, making life exciting and full of meaning. They help us understand the world and ourselves, guiding our decisions and actions.

# Purity of Heart: Navigating Emotions with Grace

Now, let's talk about purity of heart. It's like having the skill of a wise artist who can use these emotions to create a beautiful painting. Purity of heart is the ability to deal with your emotions honestly and gracefully. It doesn't mean trying to hide or deny what you feel. Instead, it's about understanding your emotions and finding a way to blend them together in a harmonious and authentic way.

Imagine you have a canvas of your own, and you want to create a masterpiece with the emotions you feel. Purity of heart is like having a clear vision of what you want to create. It's about not letting one emotion overpower the others, like not letting a single colour dominate the whole painting. It's finding a balance and using your emotions in a way that brings inner peace, clarity, and integrity.

Just like an artist mixes colours to create new shades and tones, you can navigate your emotions with grace. For example, if you feel anger, instead of lashing out or suppressing it, you can learn to express it constructively. You can mix it with understanding and empathy to create a more balanced response. This doesn't mean pretending to be someone you're not; it's about being true to yourself while also being considerate of others.

In the end, emotions are the colours that make life beautiful, and purity of heart is the artist's skill that helps you use these colours wisely. It's about creating a masterpiece out of the emotions you feel, not by denying them, but by embracing them with grace and authenticity. When you master the art of purity of heart, you can paint a life that is full of depth, beauty, and harmony.

## Manage Your Emotions

Emotions are an integral part of the human experience, influencing our thoughts, actions, and interactions with others. How we manage our emotions can significantly impact our well-being, relationships, and overall success in life. Let's explore the three primary reasons why managing emotions is of utmost importance.

## 1.  Mental and Emotional Well-being

Taking care of your mental and emotional well-being is essential for a happy and fulfilling life. The way you handle your emotions, whether they're positive or negative, can significantly impact your psychological health. Let's delve into why managing your emotions is crucial for your mental and emotional well-being.

### A. Stress Reduction:

One of the main reasons to manage your emotions is to reduce stress. Uncontrolled emotions can lead to chronic stress, which isn't good for your physical or mental health. When stress takes over, it can show up in various forms, such as anxiety, depression, or even physical health problems. By learning to manage your emotions, you can lower your stress levels and avoid the negative consequences that come with it.

Managing your emotions helps you stay calm and composed, reducing the likelihood of getting overwhelmed by stressful situations. When you're better equipped to handle your emotions, you can prevent them from taking a toll on your well-being.

## B. Enhanced Resilience:

Emotional management isn't just about controlling your feelings; it's also about building resilience. Resilience is the ability to bounce back from life's challenges, adapt to changes, and keep moving forward, no matter what life throws at you. People who are emotionally resilient are better prepared to deal with adversity and maintain their mental and emotional well-being.

Resilience helps you face setbacks and difficult situations with a positive attitude. It enables you to view challenges as opportunities for growth rather than insurmountable obstacles. This positive outlook can make a significant difference in your overall well-being.

## C. Improved Self-esteem and Self-confidence:

Your self-esteem and self-confidence are closely tied to how you manage your emotions. Uncontrolled emotions, especially negative ones like self-doubt and self-criticism, can chip away at your self-worth and self-assurance. Learning to manage these emotions can give your self-esteem a boost and help you feel more confident in yourself.

When you're better at managing your emotions, you're less likely to be dragged down by self-doubt and self-criticism. Instead, you'll be able to focus on your strengths and accomplishments, which can contribute to better mental health and greater self-assuredness.

## D. Emotional Regulation:

Emotional regulation is all about keeping your emotions in check. It's the ability to control your emotional responses, preventing outbursts and impulsive actions. When you can regulate your emotions effectively, you're more likely to have healthier relationships and experience fewer conflicts.

Having emotional regulation skills means you can handle difficult situations without reacting impulsively. This can lead to more harmonious relationships with others, as they'll see you as someone who is emotionally stable and dependable. It can also help you avoid conflicts that may have arisen due to uncontrolled emotional reactions.

## 2. Emotion Management in Building Strong Interpersonal Relationships

Positive interpersonal relationships are the cornerstone of a fulfilling life. How we handle our emotions and how we connect with others can make a world of difference in the quality of our relationships. Let's break down why emotional management is crucial for nurturing these connections.

## A. Effective Communication:

Think of effective communication as the secret sauce in any healthy relationship. People who are emotionally intelligent excel in this department. They're not only good at expressing themselves clearly but also at understanding the feelings of others. This superpower leads to conversations that are more straightforward, fewer misunderstandings, and improved conflict resolution.

When you can express yourself and listen to others effectively, you build a bridge of understanding between you and the people you care about. This bridge is essential for nurturing strong, lasting relationships.

## B. Empathy and Compassion:

Empathy, the ability to understand and share the feelings of others, is like a magic ingredient for emotional intelligence. People who manage their emotions well tend to be more empathetic and compassionate. This special sauce creates deeper, more empathic connections with others.

When you're in tune with your own emotions and can relate to the feelings of those around you, it creates bonds of understanding and warmth. Empathy and compassion are like the glue that holds strong relationships together.

## C. Conflict Resolution:

Let's face it, conflicts are a part of life, and sometimes they sneak into our relationships. Uncontrolled emotions can turn these conflicts into big battles that are tough to resolve. But when you're a master of emotional management, you're better equipped to tackle these issues with a cool head. You can engage in constructive conversations and find solutions that benefit everyone involved.

Conflict resolution is like a building block for lasting relationships. When you can navigate disagreements with grace and understanding, you're more likely to build a relationship that can withstand the test of time.

## D. Trust and Credibility:

Trust is the bedrock of any relationship. It's built on the foundation of emotional stability. People who manage their emotions consistently are seen as more trustworthy because they show reliability in their emotional responses. Trust isn't something that happens overnight; it's a result of the ongoing, steady management of emotions.

Think of trust as the roots of a strong tree, providing nourishment and stability to the relationship. When you manage your emotions well, you're watering those roots, ensuring they grow deeper and stronger.

## E. Reduced Negative Impact:

We all make mistakes, and sometimes, those mistakes can hurt others. However, when we're skilled at managing our emotions, we're less likely to lash out in the heat of the moment or act impulsively. This leads to healthier, more harmonious relationships, where the negative impact is minimized.

Picture emotional management as a safety net that keeps us from unintentionally causing emotional harm to others. It's like a shield that protects our relationships from unnecessary damage.

## 3. Emotion Management in Achieving Professional Success and Personal Growth

Emotion management isn't just about personal feelings; it's a superpower that can supercharge your career and personal development. Here's why emotional management is vital in these areas:

## A. Decision-Making and Problem-Solving:

Think of decision-making and problem-solving as the engines that drive success in the professional world. To make the best decisions and solve complex problems, you need a clear, rational mind. Emotions can cloud your judgment and lead to suboptimal outcomes. That's where emotional management comes in – it equips you with the ability to make objective, well-thought-out decisions, a skill that's incredibly valuable in your career.

When you can keep your emotions in check, you're better equipped to weigh pros and cons, consider different perspectives, and arrive at rational solutions. This quality is like a compass that guides you through the professional maze.

**B. Leadership Skills:**

Effective leadership is like a beacon that inspires and guides a team toward success. Leaders who excel often possess a high level of emotional intelligence. They can motivate and uplift their teams, create a positive work atmosphere, and gracefully navigate challenges. Leadership qualities such as empathy, resilience, and effective communication are tightly woven with emotional management.

When you master emotional management, you're more likely to connect with your team on a deeper level. You become a source of inspiration and guidance, helping your colleagues and employees thrive. It's like a magic wand that empowers you to lead by example.

**C. Adaptability and Innovation:**

In today's fast-paced world, the ability to adapt and innovate is like gold. Emotionally resilient individuals are more flexible, open to change, and better at embracing new ideas. They can also foster an environment of innovation by encouraging creativity and taking calculated risks.

When you can adapt and innovate, you're more likely to thrive in a dynamic professional landscape. You can be a driving force behind change and transformation, rather than being left behind by it. Think of it as a pair of wings that help you soar in your career.

## D. Personal Growth:

Emotional management isn't just about your job; it's a vital component of your personal growth journey. It enables you to face obstacles, learn from experiences, and continually better yourself. Emotionally intelligent individuals have an edge in setting and achieving both personal and professional goals.

When you manage your emotions effectively, you become the architect of your personal growth. You can tackle challenges with resilience and learn from your successes and failures. It's like a toolkit that equips you to build the life you want.

## E. Conflict Resolution in the Workplace:

In a professional setting, conflicts are inevitable. But how you handle them can make all the difference. Individuals who excel at emotional management are skilled in de-escalating conflicts, finding common ground, and facilitating resolutions. This paves the way for a more productive and harmonious work environment.

Conflict resolution isn't just about smoothing things over; it's about creating a positive workplace culture where differences are viewed as opportunities for growth. When you can manage your emotions during disputes, you become a peacemaker who helps your team flourish.

## Three Step Process to Manage Emotions

Let's explore the actionable three steps process to manage your emotions, this can help you to become the master of your emotional domain

### 1.  Awareness: Tuning into Your Emotions

The first step in mastering your emotions is becoming aware of them. Without awareness, you cannot effectively manage what you do not understand. Here's how to increase your emotional awareness:

**a. Find a Quiet Space:**

Create a sanctuary for yourself in the hustle and bustle of daily life. Find a quiet and comfortable place where you can focus on your inner world without distractions. This space could be your favourite nook in your home, a nearby park, or even a cozy corner in a café. By setting aside time and space for self-reflection, you can better tune into your emotions.

**b. Deep Breathing:**

Once you've settled in your quiet space, take a few moments to engage in deep, intentional breathing. Close your eyes, inhale deeply through your nose, and exhale slowly through your mouth. This simple act can help you center yourself and calm your mind, creating the perfect environment for self-discovery.

### c. Self-Reflection:

Now, it's time to dive into your emotional landscape. Begin by asking yourself a powerful question: "What am I feeling right now?" This question serves as a gateway to your inner emotional world. Try to identify the specific emotions you are experiencing. Are you feeling joy, anger, fear, sadness, or a complex mix of several emotions? As you name and claim your feelings, you begin the journey of emotional self-mastery.

## 2.  Accept: Embracing Your Emotions

The second step in managing your emotions is to accept them without judgment. It's important to remember that all emotions are natural and valid, even if they sometimes seem irrational or inconvenient. Here's how to practice acceptance:

### a. Non-Judgment:

Avoid labeling your emotions as good or bad. Emotions are neither inherently positive nor negative; they are simply signals from your inner self. Acknowledge that they are part of the human experience, and you have the right to feel whatever you feel. Non-judgment is an essential aspect of emotional intelligence.

## b. Acknowledge Emotions:

Verbalize your acceptance of your emotions. Say to yourself, "It's okay to feel this way." This affirmation can be incredibly liberating. It's a crucial step in understanding and managing your emotions effectively. Remember, you are not your emotions; you are the one experiencing them.

## 3. Action: Taking Control of Your Emotional Responses

Once you've become aware of and accepted your emotions, it's time to take action. Here are several actionable steps you can take to manage your emotions effectively:

## a. Journaling:

Writing down your emotions and the situations or thoughts that triggered them is a powerful way to gain clarity. Keeping an emotional journal can help you identify patterns and the root causes of your emotions. It's like shining a light on the emotional landscape of your life, making it easier to navigate.

## b. Mindfulness Meditation:

Mindfulness is the practice of being fully present in the moment, observing your thoughts and feelings without attachment. This technique allows you to witness your emotions without being consumed by them. During mindfulness meditation, you can focus on your breath, and as emotions arise, let them come and go like passing clouds in the sky. This practice can help you detach from your emotions, reducing their grip on your thoughts and actions.

### c. Talk to a Trusted Friend:

Sharing your emotions with a trusted friend or family member can provide valuable support and a different perspective. Sometimes, just talking about your feelings can provide relief and help you gain clarity. A trusted confidant can offer a compassionate ear and offer insights you might not have considered.

### d. Physical Release:

Emotions often manifest as physical sensations and tension in your body. Engaging in physical activities like exercise, yoga, or even taking a brisk walk can help release built-up tension and energy. Physical movement can be a powerful tool for processing and managing emotions.

### e. Positive Self-Talk:

Our internal dialogue plays a significant role in our emotional well-being. Challenge negative or self-critical thoughts with positive affirmations. Replace self-doubt with self-compassion. Instead of saying, "I'm not good enough," shift your self-talk to, "I am worthy, and I can handle this." Cultivating positive self-talk can be transformative in managing your emotions.

## f. Visualization:

Visualization is a technique that involves creating mental images to influence your emotions. When dealing with challenging emotions, you can visualize the emotion leaving your body or transforming into a more positive and constructive energy. By harnessing the power of your imagination, you can influence your emotional state positively.

## g. Choose Your Energy:

After processing your emotions, consciously choose the energy you want to embody. Decide how you want to respond to the situation or person that triggered your emotions. You have the power to shift from a reactive state to a proactive one. Choose to respond with empathy, assertiveness, or any other energy that aligns with your values and goals.

## Your Daily Check-ins : Practice Regularly: Cultivating Emotional Mastery

Emotions are a part of daily life, and mastering them is an ongoing process. The more you practice emotional leadership, the better you'll become at managing your emotions effectively. Here are some tips for incorporating emotional mastery into your daily routine:

## a. Embrace Consistency:

Make emotional awareness and management a regular part of your life. Dedicate time each day to check in with your emotions, engage in self-reflection, and practice the techniques mentioned earlier. Consistency is key to building emotional intelligence.

## b. Be Patient:

Remember that mastering your emotions is not an instant transformation but a lifelong journey. It's okay to slip up or feel overwhelmed at times. Be patient with yourself. Every step you take, no matter how small, is progress. Celebrate your victories and learn from your challenges.

## c. Set Goals:

Define specific emotional goals for yourself. What emotions do you want to become more skilled at managing? Whether it's anger, stress, anxiety, or any other emotion, setting clear goals can help you track your progress and stay motivated.

## Seek Professional Help (if needed): A Wise Decision

If you find it challenging to manage your emotions on your own, or if you are dealing with intense and persistent emotional issues, consider seeking guidance from a mental health professional. These experts are trained to provide strategies and support tailored to your specific needs. Here's how to approach seeking professional help:

## a. Self-Reflection:

Before seeking professional help, engage in some self-reflection. Consider the nature of your emotional challenges and how they impact your life. This self-awareness can help you communicate your needs effectively to a mental health professional.

**b. Research:**

Do some research to find a mental health professional who specializes in the type of emotional challenges you are facing. It's essential to find someone with the right expertise and approach

## How to cultivate Purity of Heart: A Journey to Inner Clarity and Tranquillity

"When you begin to take control of your emotions, it's an opportunity to elevate your efforts and delve into the depths of your heart. A pure heart represents a condition of inner transparency, truthfulness, and authenticity that paves the way for emotional and spiritual equilibrium. The pursuit of purity of heart is an ongoing expedition, frequently necessitating self-examination, self-awareness, and a dedicated devotion to personal development. Here are some practical steps to guide you in nurturing it."

**A quick guide to Cultivate Purity of Heart**

**1. Self-Reflection:**

- Embark on your quest for a pure heart by dedicating regular time to self-reflection. Delve deep into your thoughts, actions, and intentions.

Ask yourself profound questions such as, "Am I being completely honest with myself about my motives?" and "What are my true aspirations in this particular situation?"

— Maintain a personal journal to meticulously document your reflections. This journal becomes a treasure trove of self-discovery, allowing you to identify recurrent patterns and chart your evolution over time.

## 2. Identify and Address Negative Emotions:

— Consciously recognize and accept the presence of negative emotions, such as anger, envy, or resentment, as they surface. These emotions can cast a shadow on your heart and obstruct your pursuit of purity.

— Go a step further and explore the roots of these emotions. Are they rooted in past experiences or unresolved issues? Make it your mission to confront and heal these underlying factors, liberating your heart from their grip.

## 3. Cultivate Self-Awareness:

— Strive for an intimate understanding of your character, values, and beliefs. To purify your heart, you must be brutally honest with yourself about who you are and what you stand for.

- Harness the transformative power of mindfulness meditation, a potent tool for augmenting self-awareness. Engage in the practice of observing your thoughts and emotions without judgment, granting you a profound insight into your inner world.

## 4. Practice Forgiveness:

- Grudges and resentments act as contaminants for the heart. Cultivate the art of forgiveness, extending it not only to others but also to yourself.

- Realize that forgiveness is not a sanction for hurtful actions but a means to unburden yourself from the weight of anger and bitterness.

## 5. Cultivate Empathy:

- Empathy, the ability to comprehend and share the feelings of others, is a virtue to nurture. This involves actively listening to people, making an earnest effort to perceive the world from their vantage point, and showing compassion.

- Participate in acts of kindness and engage in volunteer work to connect with the experiences and struggles of others, thereby enriching your wellspring of empathy.

### 6. Practice Honesty:

- Honesty is the bedrock upon which purity of heart is constructed. Make a steadfast commitment to being truthful, both with yourself and with others. Eschew deceit and manipulation in your words and actions.

- Embrace honesty as a means to build trust, foster authenticity, and safeguard the integrity of your character.

### 7. Let Go of Ego:

- Ego often acts as a veil that obscures the purity of the heart. It can lead to arrogance, pride, and a self-centred approach to life.

- Cultivate humility and continually remind yourself of your fallibility. Embrace the understanding that each person is on a unique journey, and no one is superior to another.

### 8. Surround Yourself with Positivity:

- Conduct a rigorous evaluation of the people you associate with, the media you consume, and the environments you immerse yourself in. Toxic relationships and negativity can corrode the purity of your heart.

- Seek out positive, uplifting, and supportive influences. Spend your time with individuals who inspire you to become a better, kinder, and more compassionate person.

## 9. Practice Gratitude:

- Regularly express your gratitude for the blessings in your life. This practice shifts your focus from what you lack to what you have, nurturing a heart overflowing with appreciation.

- Gratitude serves as a counterbalance to negative emotions and aids in sustaining a heart that is pure and brimming with positivity.

## 10. Meditation and Mindfulness:

- Embed meditation and mindfulness practices into your daily routine. These techniques serve as anchors that keep you present, alleviate stress, and help you cultivate a profound sense of inner peace.

- Meditation permits you to detach from fleeting emotions, enabling you to connect with the serenity that resides within your heart.

## 11. Maintain a Virtuous Circle:

- Cultivating purity of heart is a perpetual journey. As you progress, revisit the preceding steps repeatedly, deepening your self-awareness and refining your intentions.

–   Always bear in mind that achieving purity of heart is not an ultimate destination but an enduring expedition of growth and self-improvement.

## Workbook Reflection Time – Life is all about powerful questioning.

1. "What's the first thing you'll do today to manage stress, stay calm, and avoid feeling overwhelmed?"

2. "What changes will you make in your personal and work life to make things better?"

3. "How can you celebrate your strengths and accept your weaknesses?"

4. "Are there stories from your past that still affect how you think today?"

5. "What helps you stay positive and focused during challenging times?"

6. "What makes you feel truly happy and fulfilled?"

7. "How can you be kinder to yourself and others every day?"

# SINCERITY OF ACTIONS

*"Let sincerity be the fuel that propels your actions, for in the authenticity of your deeds, you'll find the power to move mountains and touch hearts."*

Sincerity of actions means doing things with a true and honest intention. It's about being real and truthful in what you say and do. Sincerity is a big deal in how we live and act in many areas of life. Let's explore this idea further.

## What Is Sincerity?

Sincerity is all about being genuine. It's when you do or say something because you truly mean it. You're not pretending or being fake. Imagine someone giving you a compliment. If they mean it from the bottom of their heart, that's sincerity. But if they're just saying it to get something from you or to look good, that's insincerity.

Sincerity is like the honesty and truthfulness of your intentions. It's the opposite of deceit or manipulation. When you're sincere, you're straightforward, and your actions match your thoughts and feelings.

## Why Sincerity Matters?

In an increasingly complex and interconnected world, the value of sincerity cannot be overstated. Sincerity is not just a moral or ethical principle; it is a fundamental pillar upon which the edifice of our lives stands. Let's delves into the multifaceted importance of sincerity!

### 1. Building Trust: The Bedrock of Healthy Relationships

At the heart of sincerity lies an invaluable asset – trust. When you're sincere, people instinctively trust you. It's the knowledge that you're not attempting to deceive or manipulate them in any way. Trust serves as the bedrock of healthy relationships, spanning the spectrum from personal bonds with friends and family to the intricate web of professional connections.

Consider the workplace, for instance. In a professional setting, trust is paramount. Colleagues and superiors alike rely on the sincerity of their peers to maintain a smoothly functioning team. When one can trust that their coworkers are honest and transparent, it fosters an environment where innovation, collaboration, and collective success can thrive. In contrast, a lack of sincerity breeds suspicion and paranoia, corroding the foundation of a workplace culture.

Moreover, sincerity is equally crucial in personal relationships. In friendships, sincerity is the glue that binds individuals together. When friends know they can trust each other implicitly, it enhances the depth and resilience of their bond. In family life, trust is even more vital. Sincere communication within a family unit helps create a safe and nurturing environment for personal growth and mutual support. Without sincerity, relationships can crumble under the weight of doubt and insecurity.

## 2. Good Communication: The Gateway to Understanding

Sincerity is an indispensable ingredient for effective communication. When you are honest and straightforward in your interactions, your message becomes clear and unambiguous. This clarity reduces the likelihood of misunderstandings, misinterpretations, and confusion.

Consider the consequences of insincerity in communication. In a world where misinformation and deception can spread like wildfire, the ability to communicate sincerely is a beacon of light in the fog of disinformation. By being candid and open, you ensure that your words carry weight and meaning. This is especially important in professional contexts, where miscommunication can lead to costly mistakes, delays, and even damaged reputations.

Sincerity also plays a pivotal role in the realm of diplomacy and international relations. In negotiations between nations, for instance, honesty is often the linchpin that holds the delicate balance between cooperation and conflict. When diplomats and leaders communicate sincerely, it fosters an environment in which trust can be built, and lasting peace agreements can be achieved.

## 3.  Moral Integrity: A Guiding Light

Sincerity is not merely a pragmatic tool for better relationships and communication; it is also an embodiment of moral integrity. It reflects a strong sense of right and wrong, providing a compass to navigate the often murky waters of life's ethical dilemmas.

Individuals who consistently act with sincerity exhibit a deep commitment to their principles and values. Their words and actions align with their moral code, creating a harmony within themselves. This alignment not only offers a clear sense of direction but also serves as an inspiration to others. In a world where moral relativism can sometimes cloud the path of ethical decision-making, sincerity shines as a beacon of unwavering commitment to one's values.

Moreover, sincerity has a contagious quality. When one person acts with integrity, it encourages those around them to do the same. This ripple effect can have far-reaching consequences, contributing to the collective moral fiber of a society. As more individuals embrace sincerity as a core value, it elevates the overall moral standards of the community.

## 4.  Self-Respect: The Foundation of Self-Esteem

When you act with sincerity, you build a strong foundation of self-respect. This self-respect stems from the knowledge that you are not compromising your beliefs and values for the sake of appearances or convenience. It is the inner affirmation that you have the courage and integrity to be true to yourself.

Self-respect is a cornerstone of self-esteem. It is the unshakable belief in your worth as a person. When you consistently act with sincerity, you develop a profound sense of self-worth, which in turn bolsters your self-esteem.

Moreover, self-respect radiates outwards, influencing the way others perceive and treat you. People are naturally drawn to individuals who exude self-confidence and integrity. This magnetism can open doors to opportunities, enriching both your personal and professional life.

## 5.  Peace of Mind: The Serenity of Authenticity

Sincerity is a gateway to inner peace. It frees you from the burdens of concealing the truth or maintaining a façade. When you embrace sincerity, you can be yourself without the stress of hiding your true self.

Consider the alternative: a life shrouded in duplicity and deceit. Maintaining a façade can be mentally and emotionally exhausting. It creates a constant undercurrent of anxiety and fear, lest the façade crumbles, exposing the truth. This internal turmoil can lead to a range of psychological and physical health issues.

In contrast, when you are sincere, you experience a profound sense of liberation. You are unburdened by the need to wear masks or hide your true self. This authenticity paves the way for a peaceful and harmonious existence.

Furthermore, the peace of mind that comes with sincerity extends beyond the individual to society at large. In a world where truth and authenticity are often in short supply, individuals who embrace sincerity serve as beacons of light, offering hope and inspiration. Their actions remind us that it is possible to live a life free from the tangled web of deceit, where peace and serenity can flourish.

## Actionable Step to review your sincerity of actions.

Let's explore the Three Step Process review Your Sincerity of Actions

### Step 1: Self-Reflection

Self-reflection is the first and most crucial step in bringing W sincerity into your actions. It involves taking a close look at your own thoughts, behaviors, and motivations. This process can be as simple as setting aside some quiet time to think or keeping a journal to record your thoughts and feelings.

- **Why Self-Reflection Matters:**

Self-reflection allows you to understand the "why" behind your actions. It helps you explore your intentions, uncover hidden agendas, and reveal any insincere motivations. This introspection is essential for recognizing areas in your life where you may not be acting with sincerity.

- **How to Practice Self-Reflection:**

  1. **Find a Quiet Space:** To reflect effectively, choose a peaceful place where you won't be disturbed. This could be a cozy corner in your home, a park, or any location where you feel comfortable and at ease.

  2. **Ask Yourself Questions:** Begin by asking yourself questions like:

     - "Why am I doing this?"

     - "What are my true motivations?"

     - "Am I trying to impress someone?"

     - "Is this action aligned with my values?"

     - "Am I being honest with myself?"

  3. **Write It Down:** Consider keeping a journal to document your reflections. Writing your thoughts down can provide clarity and help you track your progress over time.

**Step 2: Honesty with Yourself**

Honesty with yourself is about being truthful and open when you identify areas of insincerity in your actions. It's okay to admit when you're not being entirely honest with yourself or others. In fact, acknowledging your insincerities is a sign of self-awareness and growth.

•   **Why Honesty with Yourself Matters:**

Honesty is key to personal growth and change. It allows you to confront the areas where you might be acting inauthentically or with insincere intentions. By being truthful with yourself, you can take steps to rectify these behaviors and move toward a more sincere way of living.

•   **How to Practice Honesty with Yourself:**

1.   **Accept Imperfections:** Understand that nobody is perfect, and everyone has moments of insincerity. It's essential to embrace these imperfections as opportunities for growth rather than viewing them as failures.

2.   **Acknowledge Insincerities:** When you discover areas where you might not be entirely sincere, acknowledge them without self-judgment. This is the first step towards positive change.

3.   **Learn from Mistakes:** Use these moments of recognition as a learning experience. Understand

why you acted insincerely and what you can do differently in the future.

## Step 3: Alignment with Values

The final step in bringing sincerity into your actions is to ensure that your behaviors align with your core values and principles. This step requires deliberate effort and consistency.

- **Why Alignment with Values Matters:**

When your actions are consistent with your values, sincerity naturally follows. You feel more genuine and truthful because you are living in harmony with what you believe in. This alignment brings a sense of purpose and fulfilment to your life.

- **How to Align Your Actions with Your Values:**

  1. **Identify Your Values:** Start by listing your core values. These are the principles that matter most to you, such as honesty, integrity, kindness, or creativity.

  2. **Prioritize Your Values:** Rank your values in order of importance. This helps you understand which values should guide your actions when there are conflicts or decisions to be made.

  3. **Make Conscious Choices:** When faced with decisions or actions, consciously refer to your

values. Ask yourself if the choice aligns with your core principles. If it doesn't, consider alternative actions that do align with your values.

4. **Practice Consistency:** Building sincerity into your actions requires ongoing practice. Be patient with yourself and consistently make choices that reflect your values.

**Workbook Reflection Time – Life is all about powerful questioning.**

1. What is my underlying motivation for this action?

2. Am I being completely honest with myself about my actions?

3. Do my actions align with my core values and beliefs?

4. Is there a discrepancy between what I say and what I do?

5. Have I considered the impact of my actions on others?

6. Am I seeking approval or validation through my actions?

7. What steps can I take to ensure greater sincerity in my actions moving forward?

# SUCCESS SHERPAS: GUIDING YOUR SUMMIT WITH MENTORS

*"Climbing the mountain of success is easier with mentors as your dedicated Sherpas, lighting the path with their wisdom and experience."*

Mentorship is a dynamic and supportive relationship in which an experienced and knowledgeable individual, known as a mentor, provides guidance, advice, and expertise to another person, known as a mentee or protege. The primary purpose of mentorship is to help the mentee develop specific skills, gain knowledge, and advance in their personal or professional life. Mentorship typically involves the transfer of wisdom, insights, and practical experiences from the mentor to the mentee, with the aim of fostering personal growth, career development, and overall success.

Mentors offer their expertise, share their experiences, and provide constructive feedback, helping the mentee set and achieve goals, make informed decisions, and overcome challenges. This relationship can be formal or informal and exists in various contexts, such as in education, the workplace, entrepreneurship, and personal development. Mentorship is a valuable way to pass down knowledge, support personal and professional growth, and establish a sense of continuity and guidance for individuals seeking to learn and grow.

Mentorship is a meaningful and dynamic concept that revolves around the development of a relationship based on shared values and beliefs, as opposed to it being merely a request for assistance or favor. In essence, it's a connection that naturally grows and evolves over time. As this relationship matures, the establishment of trust becomes a critical component, effectively turning mentorship into a two-way street where both parties engage in an exchange of knowledge and support, with the mentor guiding and assisting the mentee.

## Appreciate the Value of Mentorship as Depicted in the Epic Ramayana from India

Mentorship plays a crucial role in guiding individuals along their personal and professional journeys, offering valuable advice, wisdom, and encouragement. A classic example of mentorship from the Glorious Indian epic, the Ramayana, is the relationship between Lord Hanuman and

Jambavan. This relationship demonstrates the significance of mentorship and its role in nurturing, and unlocking hidden potential.

In the Ramayana, Lord Hanuman was tasked with crossing the vast ocean to find Mother Sita, but he initially doubted his ability to do so. Jambavan, the wise bear and King of the Himalayas, stepped in to provide guidance and motivation

He said

**"धीवर प्रसार शौर्य भरा: Dhivara, prasara shourya bhara.**

**"उतसारा स्थिरा घम्भीरा: Uthsara, stira ghambeera."**

**Translation:**

The persevering one, your bravery will take you forward.

You leap higher and higher, the one who is unshakable and determined.

These words from Jambhavan, and his mentorship helped Hanuman recognize his incredible abilities and encouraged him to overcome his self-doubt. Jambavan reminded Hanuman of his impressive achievements, such as attempting to seize the Sun, and emphasized his divine strength as the son of the God of Wind, Vayu. Fueled by this newfound self-assurance and the belief in his capabilities, Hanuman transformed into a colossal form and successfully leaped across the ocean.

**Importance of Mentorship in this Context:**

**Unleashing Hidden Potential:** Jambavan recognizes Lord Hanuman's immense capabilities, which Hanuman himself is initially unaware of. The mentor's guidance and encouragement help Hanuman discover his extraordinary strength and ability to leap across the ocean.

**Instilling Values:** Jambavan not only provides physical guidance but also imparts important values and wisdom to Lord Hanuman. This is reflected in the 'Dhivara prasar shaurya bhara sanskrti shloka,' which can be translated as "You have the prowess to accomplish the extraordinary, embrace courage, and uphold noble traditions." This mantra reinforces the significance of bravery, valor, and the importance of preserving cultural and moral values.

**Knowledge Transfer:** Jambavan's mentorship includes passing down his knowledge and experience to Hanuman. This knowledge transfer helps Hanuman not only complete the task at hand but also equips him with wisdom for future challenges.

**Encouragement and Support:** Jambavan's role as a mentor is not just about imparting skills and knowledge but also providing emotional support and motivation. His belief in Hanuman's capabilities boosts Hanuman's self-confidence.

**Legacy and Tradition:** The mentorship between Jambavan and Lord Hanuman illustrates the importance of passing on knowledge and traditions from one generation to the next.

This mentorship relationship contributes to preserving cultural heritage and values.

In the context of Hanuman and Jambavan, mentorship played a pivotal role in enabling Hanuman to overcome his doubts, realize his potential, and achieve extraordinary feats. This example serves as a powerful testament to the significance of mentorship in guiding individuals towards success and self-discovery.

## The Mentor-Mentee Relationship

The Mentor-Mentee Relationship, a dynamic that has been integral to personal and professional development for centuries, is a subject of profound significance in the realm of human interaction and self-improvement. Whether you're a seasoned professional or an aspiring novice, this relationship can offer unparalleled insights, guidance, and support. Let's explore how we delve into the essential aspects that shape this relationship: defining roles and responsibilities, building trust and rapport, and finding the right mentor or mentee.

### Defining Roles and Responsibilities

One of the foundational elements of a successful mentor-mentee relationship is the clear definition of roles and responsibilities. Like cogs in a well-oiled machine, mentors and mentees must understand their respective functions in the partnership.

Mentors, often possessing wisdom and experience, take on the role of a guide, offering their insights and knowledge to their mentees. They provide valuable advice, share their own experiences, and create a supportive environment for growth. The mentor's responsibility lies in being a source of inspiration, offering constructive feedback, and helping the mentee set and achieve goals. Their role is that of a trusted advisor, offering both professional and personal guidance.

On the other side of the coin, mentees have their own set of responsibilities. They must approach the relationship with an open mind and a willingness to learn. It's crucial for mentees to actively seek guidance and actively participate in their own growth and development. They should ask questions, seek feedback, and be open to constructive criticism. In this relationship, accountability is a shared responsibility. Mentees must strive to make the most of their mentor's expertise.

## Building Trust and Rapport

Trust and rapport are the building blocks of a robust mentor-mentee relationship. Without them, the connection can crumble, leaving both parties feeling unsatisfied and unfulfilled. Trust is the bedrock upon which a meaningful mentorship is established. Both the mentor and the mentee must be confident that the other has their best interests at heart.

To build trust, communication is key. Open, honest, and confidential conversations are vital. A mentor should create an environment where a mentee feels safe discussing their goals, challenges, and even their failures. Mentees, in turn, should respect the mentor's time and expertise and honor the trust placed in them.

Rapport is the emotional connection that adds a personal touch to the mentor-mentee relationship. It's the camaraderie, the shared experiences, and the understanding that transcends mere professional interaction. Building rapport can be as simple as taking a few minutes before or after formal meetings to discuss personal interests, hobbies, or life experiences. These small interactions can help forge a connection beyond the mentorship's official boundaries, making the relationship more enjoyable and enduring.

## Finding the Right Mentor or Mentee

Finding the right mentor or mentee is a crucial step in establishing a successful partnership. The process may seem daunting, but with some strategic considerations, you can identify an ideal match.

### Where to Look

The first step in finding the right mentor or mentee is to identify where to look. In the professional realm, your workplace is often a primary source. Within your organization, you may find experienced colleagues who can provide invaluable guidance. Alternatively, industry events, conferences, and professional networking organizations can be excellent places to meet potential mentors or mentees. Online platforms, such as LinkedIn, can also be a rich source for identifying suitable candidates. Beyond the professional sphere, you can explore your personal network, including friends and family, to discover mentorship possibilities.

Moreover, don't underestimate the power of specialized mentorship programs. Many educational institutions and organizations offer structured mentorship programs that can help you find the right fit. These programs often facilitate the initial connection and provide a framework for the mentorship relationship to thrive.

## Qualities to Seek

When searching for the right mentor or mentee, it's essential to consider the qualities you seek in a potential partner. These qualities can vary depending on your personal and professional goals, but some universal traits are worth seeking.

For mentors, experience is undoubtedly valuable. Look for individuals who have navigated a path similar to the one you're on, with a track record of success. The ability to communicate effectively, provide constructive feedback, and show patience are also critical mentor qualities. Mentors should be committed to your growth and willing to invest time and effort into the relationship.

Mentees, on the other hand, should seek mentors who are not only experienced but also willing to share their knowledge and insights. Look for someone who is genuinely interested in your development and has the ability to provide constructive feedback. A mentee should also be open to constructive criticism and able to act on the mentor's guidance.

Furthermore, shared values and goals are vital for a harmonious mentor-mentee relationship. Having aligned objectives and a shared vision can make the partnership more fruitful and fulfilling. Both parties should be committed to the mentorship's success, and their values should resonate with one another.

## Handling Conflict and Misalignment

Mentorship is a fantastic way for people to learn and grow, both personally and professionally. It's like having a guide who helps you become better at something, whether it's a job, a skill, or just life in general. But, like any relationship, mentorships can have problems too. Let's explore how to deal with disagreements, handle different expectations, and work through differences in age and culture in the mentorship.

## Addressing Disagreements

Disagreements are normal in any relationship, even in mentorships. When you and your mentor don't see eye to eye on something, it's essential to deal with it in a positive way. Ignoring these conflicts can make things worse, and it can slow down your progress.

A good way to handle disagreements is by talking openly. Both you and your mentor should feel comfortable expressing your concerns and frustrations. When problems come up, focus on finding a solution, not blaming each other. Sometimes, if things get really tough, you might need a neutral third party, like a mediator or someone from HR, to help you find a solution. The main goal is to work things out and keep your mentorship going in a good and productive direction.

## Managing Differences in Expectations

Expectations are like what you hope to get out of your mentorship. It's important that both you and your mentor are on the same page about what you expect. This means talking honestly at the beginning about things like what you want to learn, how often you'll meet, and what you hope to achieve.

It's crucial that both sides are realistic. If your expectations are too big or not doable, you might end up disappointed. The key is to set clear, realistic goals and keep talking to make sure they still make sense as you go along in your mentorship.

## Navigating Generational and Cultural Differences

In mentorships, you and your mentor might come from different generations or cultures, which can be a good thing, but it can also lead to misunderstandings and conflicts.

### Bridging Gaps

To bridge these gaps, it's important to be open-minded and empathetic. This means being willing to see things from the other person's point of view. If you're the mentor, you should be open to changing the way you mentor to fit what your mentee needs. Younger people often have different ideas and ways of doing things. And if you're the mentee, you should respect your mentor's experience and what they can teach you. It's about finding a balance and learning from each other.

## Measuring the Impact of Mentorship

Mentorship is a dynamic and transformational relationship, a mutual exchange of wisdom and support that leaves an indelible mark on both mentors and mentees. Lets delve into the realm of mentorship, exploring how to evaluate its impact, savor its enduring rewards, and highlight the essence of guiding the next generation of mentors.

Measuring the success of mentorship is akin to capturing a fleeting breeze—subtle yet profound. The true fruits of mentorship often ripen long after the formal relationship ends. Nevertheless, there exists a spectrum of vital indicators that shed light on the success of mentorship, encompassing various facets that span from achievement and personal growth to feedback and community engagement.

**1. Achievement of Goals :** A fundamental yardstick of mentorship success lies in the mentee's progress towards their set objectives. Whether the mentee's ambitions revolve around career advancement, skill enhancement, or personal growth, these tangible achievements serve as a beacon, illuminating the efficacy of the mentorship. When a mentee strides closer to their goals, it not only reflects their commitment but also underscores the mentor's capacity to guide and support.

**2. Personal Growth :** Another critical indicator of a successful mentorship is the mentee's personal development. As the mentorship progresses, mentees often experience a transformation in their self-esteem and self-image. The mentor's guidance, encouragement, and insights contribute to this metamorphosis, fostering a more confident and self-assured individual. The increased self-esteem, coupled with a constructive self-image, can be considered a direct product of a successful mentorship.

**3. Feedback and Evaluation :** Effective mentorship relies on a continuous exchange of feedback between the mentor and mentee. This ongoing evaluation acts as a compass, steering the mentorship towards success. Honest and constructive communication not only identifies areas for improvement but also cultivates an environment of growth and trust. A mentor who can provide guidance and support while also welcoming feedback is more likely to guide their mentee towards success.

**4. Mentee Satisfaction :** An essential aspect of measuring mentorship success is gauging the mentee's satisfaction with the relationship. Are the mentee's needs being met? Are they reaping the intended benefits from the mentorship? A contented mentee is more likely to stay engaged and committed to the mentorship, and their satisfaction is a testament to the mentor's ability to offer valuable support and guidance.

**5. Mentor Satisfaction :** Similarly, the mentor's satisfaction is pivotal in evaluating the success of mentorship. It's not just about the mentee's progress but also about whether the mentor is fulfilled and witnessing the transformative impact they aspired to create. A mentor who finds personal and professional fulfilment in guiding their mentee is more likely to provide unwavering support, thereby enhancing the chances of mentorship success.

**6. Longevity of Relationship :** When a mentorship transcends its initial duration and evolves into a long-term partnership, it signifies a resounding success. The enduring nature of the relationship is a testament to the value it continues to bring to both mentor and mentee. Longevity reflects the continued growth and development stemming from the mentorship, and it underlines the positive impact it has on both the personal and professional lives of those involved.

**7. Community and Network Engagement**: An often underestimated but crucial aspect of mentorship success is the mentee's integration into the mentor's professional network and the broader community. The depth of this integration serves as an indicator of the mentorship's impact. A mentee who actively engages with the mentor's network not only expands their own opportunities but also reaffirms the mentor's role as a valuable guide. Furthermore, this community and network engagement can create a ripple effect, potentially leading to more significant opportunities for the mentee and solidifying the mentor's influence in their field.

Mentorship is an indispensable force that transcends all aspects of life, particularly in nurturing the potential of our youth. It is through mentorship that the flame of inspiration is ignited, and the path to greatness illuminated. As we journey through life, let us recognize the profound significance of mentorship, for it is the catalyst that propels us towards our dreams, offers guidance when we falter, and instills in us the belief that our aspirations are within reach. So, let us continue to embrace the transformative power of mentorship, for it is not merely a support system, but a beacon of hope that lights the way to a brighter, more fulfilling future.

# AWAKENING THE SPIRITUALLY CONSCIOUS YOUTH



Spirituality, a multifaceted and intricate concept, finds its definition subject to considerable variation contingent on cultural, religious, and individual perspectives. The essence of spirituality, to me, typically encapsulates a profound and intimate sense of being interconnected with an entity or force beyond one's immediate self. This profound connection can manifest in a multitude of forms, spanning the belief in a higher power, an overarching universal energy, the harmonious resonance with the natural world, or an intrinsic sense of purpose and meaning residing within one's inner self. It often embarks upon a profound quest to fathom the deeper enigmas of existence and embarks on an exploration of one's inner self and consciousness.

One of the fundamental characteristics of spirituality is its inherent subjectivity. What constitutes a spiritual experience for one person may not hold the same significance for another. The diversity of perspectives on spirituality is both its strength and its challenge. This diversity enables individuals to personalize their spiritual journeys, tailoring their beliefs and practices to their unique experiences, needs, and desires. However, it can also lead to conflict and misunderstanding when these subjective experiences clash with one another.

The pursuit of spirituality often involves a relentless quest to penetrate the veils of existence. It beckons individuals to embark on a journey of self-discovery, encouraging them to peel back the layers of their own consciousness and explore the deeper mysteries that lie beneath the surface. This journey delves into the very heart of what it means to be human, prompting us to ask profound questions about our place in the cosmos, the nature of our existence, and the purpose that drives us forward.

Embarking on a journey of self-discovery is a daunting path, fraught with myriad challenges and the risk of becoming lost in the labyrinthine corridors of one's own psyche. It is in such precarious moments that religion often emerges as a guiding light, illuminating the way for those seeking to navigate the labyrinth of self.

Religion, in contrast to the highly personalized nature of spirituality, often provides a structured framework with established beliefs, rituals, and moral guidelines. These structures can offer a sense of stability and direction to individuals seeking to explore their spirituality. Religious traditions offer a well-trodden path, complete with maps, signposts, and a community of fellow travelers. This can be immensely reassuring to those who may feel lost or adrift on their spiritual journey.

The role of religion in the context of spirituality is not to be underestimated. For many people, religion provides a sense of belonging and community. It offers a ready-made support system of like-minded individuals who share common beliefs and values. This sense of belonging can be comforting and provide a profound sense of connection to something greater than oneself, just as spirituality does.

Religion can also provide a moral compass, offering clear guidelines for ethical behavior and decision-making. It can help individuals navigate the complex moral landscape of life by providing a set of principles and doctrines that align with their spiritual beliefs. This can be particularly important when facing challenging ethical dilemmas or seeking guidance in making important life choices.

In addition to offering structure, community, and moral guidance, religion often addresses the existential questions that are at the heart of the spiritual journey. It provides answers, or at least attempts to, to questions about the nature of the divine, the afterlife, the purpose of existence, and the origin of the universe. These answers can provide a sense of certainty and security for those who seek them.

## Challenges and resilience for youth in spiritual consciousness

Challenges and resilience for youth in spiritual consciousness are multifaceted and complex. Spirituality refers to a deeply personal and subjective connection to a higher power, a sense of purpose, and an exploration of life's meaning. Young people often grapple with these issues, and while spirituality can provide a source of strength and resilience, it can also present challenges. Here's a detailed exploration of these challenges and the role of resilience in navigating them:

### Challenges:

1. **Identity and Belonging:** Youth may struggle with their spiritual identity, especially if they come from a diverse religious or non-religious background. They may question their beliefs, wonder where they fit in, or feel alienated if their spirituality is different from their peers.

2. **Peer Pressure:** Many young people face peer pressure to conform to certain beliefs or practices. They may feel pressured to engage in behaviors or lifestyles that conflict with their spiritual values.

3. **Skepticism and Doubt:** As adolescents and young adults develop critical thinking skills, they often question their faith or spirituality. Doubt and skepticism can be challenging to navigate and may lead to existential crises.

4. **Cultural and Social Differences:** Cultural and social factors can influence a person's spiritual beliefs. Young people may struggle to reconcile their spirituality with the norms and expectations of their culture or society.

5. **Mental Health:** Youth may experience mental health challenges like anxiety and depression, which can affect their spiritual well-being. They might question why they are suffering or feel disconnected from their spirituality during difficult times.

6. **Religious Extremism and Fundamentalism:** In some cases, youth may be exposed to extreme or fundamentalist religious ideologies, which can be harmful and divisive. This can challenge their ability to engage with spirituality in a healthy and balanced way.

## Resilience:

1. **Self-Exploration:** Resilient youth engage in self-reflection and exploration of their spirituality. They take the time to understand their beliefs, values, and what gives their life meaning.

2. **Open-mindedness:** Resilience often involves being open to diverse perspectives and beliefs. Youth who are resilient are willing to learn from others and adapt their spiritual views if needed.

3. **Support Networks:** Building a support network of friends, family, or mentors who respect and encourage their spiritual journey is crucial for resilience. Having people to talk to and lean on can help young people navigate challenges.

4. **Education:** Resilient youth invest in learning about various spiritual and religious traditions. They seek knowledge and develop a broader perspective, which can help them make informed decisions about their own spirituality.

5. **Mental Health Awareness:** Resilience includes recognizing the importance of mental health and seeking help when needed. Mindfulness practices, meditation, or therapy can help young people maintain their spiritual well-being during difficult times.

6. **Community Engagement:** Being part of a spiritual community or group can offer support and a sense of belonging. Resilient youth often find strength in connecting with like-minded individuals who share their beliefs.

7. **Adaptability:** Resilience in spirituality involves the ability to adapt to changing circumstances

and challenges. It means understanding that one's spiritual journey may evolve and transform over time.

## Key Aspects of Spiritual Consciousness

Spiritual consciousness is a deeply personal and subjective experience that varies from person to person. While it's challenging to provide a one-size-fits-all definition, there are key aspects that can be relevant to many youth exploring their spiritual consciousness. Here are some key aspects of spiritual consciousness for youth, explained in detail:

1. **Self-Exploration:**

   - **Definition:** This involves an introspective journey to understand one's inner self, beliefs, values, and purpose in life. It's about asking fundamental questions about one's existence and seeking answers from within.

   - **Significance for Youth:** Self-exploration allows young individuals to discover their unique spiritual identity. It empowers them to form a strong foundation for their beliefs and values, which can guide their life choices.

2. **Meaning and Purpose:**

   - **Definition:** This aspect involves seeking a deeper sense of meaning and purpose in life beyond the superficial or material aspects. It often leads to questions about the significance of one's actions and existence.

- **Significance for Youth:** Youth are at a stage in life where they're searching for meaning and purpose. Spiritual consciousness can provide a framework for understanding and pursuing these existential questions.

## 3. Connection to a Higher Power or Transcendence:

- **Definition:** This aspect encompasses belief in, and a connection to, a higher power, whether it's a traditional deity, the universe, or a transcendent force. It's about feeling a connection beyond the material world.

- **Significance for Youth:** This can offer solace and comfort, particularly during difficult times. It provides a sense of guidance and support, which is essential for emotional well-being in youth.

## 4. Values and Ethics:

- **Definition:** Spiritual consciousness often leads to the development of a set of values and ethical principles that guide one's behavior and decision-making. It's about living in alignment with one's beliefs.

- **Significance for Youth:** Young people are forming their moral compass during this stage. Spiritual consciousness helps them make ethical decisions, promotes empathy, and encourages them to contribute positively to society.

5.  **Compassion and Empathy:**

    -   **Definition:** This aspect involves a deep sense of compassion and empathy towards oneself and others. It's about recognizing the interconnectedness of all beings and responding with kindness.

    -   **Significance for Youth:** Youth exploring spiritual consciousness are encouraged to develop greater empathy and compassion. This can lead to improved relationships and a more harmonious society.

6.  **Mindfulness and Presence:**

    -   **Definition:** Practicing mindfulness and being present in the moment is a significant aspect of spiritual consciousness. It involves cultivating awareness and focus on the here and now.

    -   **Significance for Youth:** Mindfulness can help youth manage stress and anxiety, improve their concentration, and enhance their overall well-being. It encourages them to appreciate life's simple moments.

7.  **Seeking Truth and Knowledge:**

    -   **Definition:** Spiritual consciousness often involves a quest for truth and knowledge. It encourages individuals to learn from various sources, engage in critical thinking, and expand their understanding of the world.

- **Significance for Youth:** This aspect can lead to personal growth and a broader perspective on life. It helps young people become more open-minded and better equipped to make informed decisions.

## 8. Community and Fellowship:

- **Definition:** Many spiritual journeys involve a sense of community and fellowship with like-minded individuals. This can be through religious congregations, spiritual groups, or supportive networks.

- **Significance for Youth:** Being part of a community provides youth with a support system, a sense of belonging, and opportunities for shared growth and learning.

## 9. Transcending Materialism:

- **Definition:** Spiritual consciousness often encourages individuals to look beyond materialism and find value in non-material aspects of life, such as relationships, experiences, and inner peace.

- **Significance for Youth:** This aspect can help youth resist the pressure of consumerism and materialism, promoting a more balanced and fulfilling life.

## Spiritual Practices for Youth

Spiritual practices for youth should be actionable, accessible, and relevant to their age and stage of life. These practices can help young individuals explore and cultivate their spiritual consciousness. Here are some actionable spiritual practices for youth, explained in detail:

**1. Meditation and Mindfulness:**

- **Practice:** Meditation involves sitting quietly, focusing on one's breath or a specific object, and clearing the mind of distractions. Mindfulness is about being fully present in the moment and observing one's thoughts and feelings without judgment.

- **Significance:** Meditation and mindfulness help youth become more self-aware, reduce stress and anxiety, and foster a sense of inner peace. They encourage living in the present moment, which is essential for spiritual growth.

- **Action Steps:**

  i. Set aside a specific time each day for meditation or mindfulness.

  ii. Find a quiet, comfortable space to sit or lie down.

   iii.  Focus on your breath, a mantra, or an object.

   iv.  When distractions arise, gently bring your attention back to the chosen focus.

   v.  Start with a few minutes daily and gradually increase the duration as you become more comfortable.

## 2. Journaling:

- **Practice:** Journaling involves writing down your thoughts, feelings, and reflections on your spiritual journey, experiences, and questions.

- **Significance:** Journaling provides a safe and structured way for youth to explore their spiritual experiences, gain clarity, and track their personal growth and insights.

- **Action Steps:**

   i.  Set aside a regular time for journaling.

   ii.  Write freely about your spiritual experiences, doubts, and questions.

   iii.  Reflect on your values, beliefs, and any personal growth you've experienced.

   iv.  Use your journal to set intentions and track your progress in your spiritual journey.

3. **Acts of Kindness and Service:**

   - **Practice:** Engage in acts of kindness and service to others, whether it's volunteering, helping a friend in need, or practicing random acts of kindness.

   - **Significance:** Acts of kindness and service promote compassion, empathy, and a sense of interconnectedness. They embody the spiritual principle of selflessness and contribute to a more meaningful life.

   - **Action Steps:**

     i. Identify opportunities to help others in your community or among your peers.

     ii. Volunteer at a local charity or nonprofit organization.

     iii. Practice daily acts of kindness, such as complimenting someone or offering assistance when needed.

4. **Study of Sacred Texts and Literature:**

   - **Practice**: Explore and study sacred texts, spiritual literature, or philosophical writings that resonate with your beliefs or interests.

   - **Significance:** The study of sacred texts and spiritual literature can deepen your understanding of your faith or spirituality, provide guidance, and offer insights into life's meaning and purpose.

- **Action Steps:**

    i. Start by selecting a text or book that aligns with your spiritual interests.

    ii. Set aside regular time for reading and reflection.

    iii. Take notes, underline key passages, and contemplate the teachings within the text.

    iv. Discuss what you've learned with mentors, peers, or a study group.

## 5. Nature Connection:

- **Practice:** Spend time in nature, whether it's hiking, camping, gardening, or simply taking a walk in the park.

- **Significance:** Connecting with nature can provide a sense of awe and wonder, reminding youth of the beauty and interconnectedness of all life. It can also promote inner peace and spiritual reflection.

- **Action Steps:**

    i. Plan regular outings or activities in natural settings.

    ii. Be mindful of the natural world, its beauty, and its intricate balance.

iii.  Reflect on the connection between nature and your own spiritual beliefs.

iv.  Practice gratitude for the natural world and its role in your spiritual journey.

## 6. Prayer:

- **Practice:** Prayer involves communicating with a higher power, expressing gratitude, seeking guidance, or simply engaging in a conversation with the divine. Prayer can be formal or informal and can take various forms, such as reciting scripted prayers, speaking from the heart, or using meditation and reflection as a form of prayer.

- **Significance:** Prayer is a way for youth to establish a personal connection with their spiritual beliefs, a higher power, or the divine. It offers a means of seeking support, expressing gratitude, and finding solace during challenging times.

- **Action Steps:**

  - **Set a Prayer Routine:** Designate specific times in your day for prayer, whether it's in the morning, before meals, or before bedtime. Consistency in your routine can help prayer become a regular part of your spiritual practice.

- **Choose Your Prayer Style:** Decide whether you want to use scripted prayers from your religious tradition or engage in more informal, spontaneous conversations with the divine. You can also use meditation techniques to center your thoughts and engage in silent contemplative prayer.

- **Express Gratitude:** Start your prayers by expressing gratitude for the blessings in your life. This can help cultivate a positive mindset and foster a sense of thankfulness.

- **Seek Guidance:** If you have questions or uncertainties, prayer can be a way to seek guidance, clarity, or strength to overcome challenges. Ask for insight and wisdom during your prayer sessions.

- **Pray for Others:** Include in your prayers not only personal concerns but also the well-being of others, especially those in need. This practice promotes compassion and a sense of interconnectedness.

- **Create a Sacred Space:** Designate a quiet and peaceful space where you can engage in prayer. It could be a corner of your room, a garden, or any place where you feel spiritually connected.

Prayer is a versatile and deeply personal practice that can offer youth a sense of connection, purpose, and guidance in their spiritual exploration. Whether through traditional religious rituals or more free-form expressions, prayer can be a valuable component of their spiritual consciousness.

These actionable spiritual practices for youth can be incorporated into daily life and tailored to individual preferences and beliefs. They provide a foundation for self-exploration, personal growth, and the development of a deeper spiritual consciousness.

**Workbook Reflection Time – Life is all about powerful questioning.**

1.  How do you connect with the sacred or the divine, if at all?

2.  What are your core values and beliefs?

3.  Do you have a regular spiritual practice or routine?

4.  How do you navigate challenges and adversity from a spiritual perspective?

5.  In what ways do you show compassion and empathy to others and to yourself?

6.  What role does gratitude play in your life?

7.  Are you involved in any form of community or fellowship that supports your spiritual journey?

8.  How do you reconcile doubts or skepticism with your spiritual beliefs?

9.  What actions or practices help you feel more connected to the world and the people around you?

# CONCLUSION

In the midst of life's many distractions, creating our unique path might seem challenging, but it's entirely possible. To do this, we need clear thinking, a kind heart, genuine actions, and a spiritual connection. By combining these elements, our lives become more meaningful.

As we conclude our journey through the pages of "Vividly You(th)," I am reminded of the profound wisdom encapsulated in the timeless verses of India's venerable Prime Minister, Atal Bihari Vajpayee:

> "जन्म-मरण का खेल अनूठा, इसमें हार नहीं है,
> वो क्या चल पाएगा, जिसको पथ से प्यार नहीं है
> "पथ पर चलते चलते ही वह राह बन गया,
> तिल-तिल कर जलते जलते ही दाह बन गया,
> वह कैसा था भक्त स्वयं भगवान बन गया
> कुम्भकार की कीर्ति बन निर्माण बन गया!"

**Translation**

"The game of birth and death is unique, there is no defeat in it. What can one achieve, who does not love the path?

"While walking on the path, it became the way itself, turning to ashes bit by bit, What kind of devotee was he, who became God himself, the potter's glory turned into creation!"

## Meaning

"Life's journey is a unique game, where you can't lose. Those who love their path will find success. The path is created as we walk it, and challenges make us stronger. By seeking our true selves, we can achieve something divine, leaving a lasting legacy."

In the context of youth, these verses unveil profound insights:

**In the context of youth, this poem can be understood as follows:**

**Path of Self-Discovery:** The journey of life is a complex and multifaceted expedition that each young person embarks on. It's a journey filled with questions and uncertainties, a quest to find one's purpose and direction. The poem beautifully suggests that the path of self-discovery is not something preordained or immediately clear. Instead, it becomes apparent as you keep moving forward. This concept is profoundly reassuring, as it implies that the act of living, experiencing, and learning is what ultimately forges the path.

As young individuals, we often find ourselves at crossroads, facing choices that can seem daunting. The path may seem obscured, shrouded in uncertainty, much like a dark forest awaiting illumination. But the poem teaches us that it's the very act of taking the first step, and then the next, that gradually illuminates the way. Every experience, whether positive or negative, contributes to shaping the path we tread.

**Overcoming Challenges:** The journey of youth is often characterized by challenges and difficulties. The reference in the poem, "til-til kar jalte jalte hi daha ban gaya," is a powerful metaphor for the transformative nature of these hardships. Just as gold is subjected to intense heat and pressure to become purer, so too do young people emerge stronger and wiser when they confront life's trials.

Youth must face numerous challenges on their path— educational struggles, personal setbacks, emotional turmoil, and societal pressures. These challenges can feel like flames licking at their very being, but just as gold endures the crucible of fire and emerges brighter and more valuable, so do young individuals mature and become more resilient through their trials. Challenges, rather than obstacles, become stepping stones in their journey. They serve as opportunities for growth, teaching essential life lessons that shape character and wisdom.

**Self-Realization and Spirituality:** The lines "वह कैसा था भक्त स्वयं भगवान बन गया" carry profound implications for self-realization and spirituality. They signify that those who earnestly seek their path, who delve into self-discovery with devotion and sincerity, can ultimately realize their true potential and connect with a higher spiritual purpose.

The transformation from a simple seeker to one who embodies divinity is a profound journey of inner growth and enlightenment.

For many young people, spirituality and self-realization are vital aspects of their journey. This journey often involves questioning the meaning of life, exploring one's beliefs, and searching for a deeper connection with the universe. The poem suggests that, like a devout follower who evolves into a divine being, young individuals can transcend their limited perceptions and become conduits of higher wisdom and understanding. This spiritual evolution is an essential component of self-discovery and growth, enabling them to navigate life's challenges with grace and equanimity.

**Building a Legacy:** The concluding line of the poem, "कुम्भकार की कीर्ति बन निर्माण बन गया," carries a profound message about building a legacy. It underscores the idea that through dedication and determination, young people can leave a lasting imprint on the world. The analogy of a potter molding and creating beautiful pottery emphasizes the power of deliberate effort in shaping one's destiny.

Every young person aspires to make a mark, to be remembered for their contributions to the world. However, this journey is not merely about personal success; it's about leaving behind something of value that benefits others and enriches the tapestry of humanity. Just as a potter crafts each piece of pottery with precision and care, young individuals can shape their lives with intention, creating something beautiful and lasting. It's a reminder that the pursuit of excellence and the dedication to one's chosen path can lead to a legacy that endures through generations.

In closing, these verses serve as a poignant reminder that the pursuit of purpose is an ever-unfolding journey. They inspire youth to persist, to find strength in adversity, to connect with their inner selves, and to aspire to leave behind a legacy that resonates through the ages. "Vividly You(th)" encourages the young and the young at heart to embrace this timeless wisdom and embark on their quest to unveil their own divine design amidst the clamor of the world. With clarity, purity, sincerity, and spirituality as their guiding stars, they shall illuminate the world with their brilliance, embodying the eternal spirit of self-discovery and purpose.

Happy Reading

Anurag Sharma

# ABOUT THE AUTHOR

Anurag Sharma boasts an impressive 15-year track record, standing out as both a seasoned Management Consultant and Product Manager who consistently delivers strategic solutions to intricate business challenges across a multitude of industries. Anurag's central mission revolves around guiding organizations in the creation and management of products that hold a profound impact on people's lives.

Beyond their managerial prowess, Anurag Sharma shines as a proficient leader in steering organizational change, optimizing processes, and enhancing performance. Their forte extends to data-driven decision-making, expertly managing stakeholders, and possessing a profound grasp of product management.

Anurag's passion extends to being a dedicated Performance Coach and Mentor, where they diligently nurture the human core to instill a Growth mindset within organizations, securing the sustainable delivery of value to their customers.

In addition to their impressive professional journey, Anurag is a prolific author, contributing to impactful books including "You can Impact," (Co-Authored) "Test Environment Management," and "A Concise Introduction to Digital Transformation." Moreover, Anurag is a highly skilled speaker who generously shares their wealth of knowledge and profound insights with a diverse and appreciative audience.

**Instagram:** @coachanurag

**LinkedIn:** https://www.linkedin.com/in/anuragsharmapro/